TERRY SCHMIDA'S
TRUE CRIME Vol 2
STORIES OF KEY WEST AND THE FLORIDA KEYS

Don't end up in Vol. III!

— Terry Schmida

Copyright © 2008 Key West Crook Books, LLC.

All rights reserved. Unauthorized duplication is a violation of applicable laws

"True Crime Stories of Key West and the Florida Keys" is a trademark for books in a series, so don't even think about writing one in your town, unless you buy the rights from us.

Please address inquiries to Terry Schmida at keysscribe@aol.com.

Cover design: Wodu Media.
Cover photos: Rob O'Neal, www.roboneal.com.
Design and production: Marc Phelps.

Rare first edition. Buy several copies!

10 9 8 7 6 5 4 3
ISBN 978-0-615-24400-6

CONTENTS

Acknowledgements 5

Introduction 6

Jailbreak! 8

Rough Justice 16

The Mile High Club 24

The First Execution 30

On the Down Low 36

He Was Expendable 42

Deadliest Catch 50

The Castanon-Reyes Affair 58

America's Most Wanted 64

Killed By the Klan 72

A Short Fuse 80

One Count of Weirdness 90

The "Bubba Bust" 98

End of the Rainbow 110

The Shocking Death of Judge Aquilino Lopez 122

About the Author 126

Thank you, your honors . . .

First off, as always, thank YOU for buying this book. You're helping to keep Key West writers at our keyboards, and away from committing petty crime to pay our bills. The customer is always Chief.

Troopers include my parents, Walter and Joanna Schmida, whose limitless love, support and sheer braininess have been a constant source of inspiration to me over the years. This book is for both of you.

Historian Tom Hambright would be a Ranger. As the history-obsessed guardian of Florida history at the Key West branch of the Monroe County Library, Tom has contributed so much to so many books about the Keys that I think it's time we created a statue in his honor.

Officers of the court include former Solares Hill editor Nancy Klingener; Canadian motivators Max Haines and Amy Cormier; deranged but brilliant cover designer Peter Downie; layout artist Marc Phelps; local literary boosters Tom Corcoran, Michael Haskins, George Cooper, and Rick Worth; proof-reader and babe Stephanie Hellstrom; local radio and TV star (and old friend) Bill Hoebee; Erin and Mary Bäcker; and our gorgeous cover model, Christa Hunt of Key West Burlesque. (Don't miss her fantastic show while you're in town: www.keywestburlesque.com.)

My partners in crime include Key West writer/entrepreneur/publishing guru David L. Sloan; my longtime friend, supporter and proof-reader Mandy Bolen; and my best friend and colleague Rob O'Neal. I couldn't have done this without you guys.

Mad love to you all!

And special thanks to the countless others out there who have helped, challenged and encouraged me in the creation of this project. You are in this book.

To Ken Hock for letting it slide . . . .

Introduction

Greetings true crime readers, and . . . welcome to my sequel!

Since I published *True Crime Vol. 1* in September of 2006, I've been overwhelmed by the response. The book is now a Florida Keys bestseller, with many thousands of copies sold.

Researching and writing about local crime began as a hobby – inspired by *Toronto Sun* Crime Flashback columnist Max Haines. It is now a passion and part-time job.

Thanks to my first book's success I've been privileged to discuss true crime at signing parties, radio and television shows, and Friends of the Library gatherings up and down the Keys.

Perhaps inevitably, I've been approached by many people with their own tales to tell. Some folks shared off-the-record secrets about their family and friends; others just wanted to make me aware of past cases that hadn't been included in *Vol. 1*. All of them asked the same question: "When are you gonna come out with another crime book?"

The answer is: Now.

Almost from the moment I finished writing the first edition, I KNEW I'd be putting together a sequel. There were just too many interesting stories I didn't have room for in *Vol. 1*. Other cases were brought to my attention by friends such as local historian Tom Hambright at the Key West branch of the Monroe County Library. Happily, I discovered that the treasure trove of largely forgotten history I mined the first time around still had plenty left to offer. I can honestly say that the material in this new book more than holds its own with the contents of its predecessor. Both volumes complement each other nicely and needn't be read in the order they were written.

One difference between the two books is that the stories in this volume tend to be of a more recent vintage. This is one of the ways I consider the sequel an appropriate fit with the mostly older tales in

Vol. 1. As before, however, care has been taken, not to revive painful memories for the victims of the crimes – or their families.

So lock up your doors, dim the lights and prepare to embark on a journey into the darker side of paradise . . . a place where anything can happen anytime – and often does.

Terry Schmida,
Key West, Florida, June 2008

True Crime Stories of Key West and the Florida Keys, Vol. 2

Photo by roboneal.com

Old comics and county records occupy a bunk at the old Monroe County Jail on Whitehead Street.

Jailbreak!

The old jail couldn't contain dangerous killers like the Bonvillion brothers. Not for long, anyways . . . .

"Hellhole."

That was a common description of the "old" Monroe County Jail, given by inmates and guards alike. From its dedication in 1967 to its demise 26 years later, the jail, located on the second floor of the Jefferson B. Browne Courthouse Annex building on Whitehead Street, truly was a dungeon of the damned.

Riots. Fires. Overcrowding. Filthy conditions. The place didn't even have air conditioning until 1985. The lock-up was a 1920s Texas jail that was floated to Key West on barges and reassembled in the courthouse building. It had been designed for an era when prisoners were better behaved and so was hugely ill-suited for the increasingly violent, drug-addled Florida Keys inmates of the 1970s, '80s and '90s.

Prisoners would back up their toilets to flood the courtrooms and offices below and set fires in cellblocks that were already hazy with cigarette smoke. They'd reach through their cell bars to grab the guards as they patrolled corridors that were just 30-inches wide between the two rows of cells.

Worst of all, for Key Westers, was the ease with which resourceful inmates were able to escape. For a brief period in the early 1980s, it appeared that prisoners – or some of them – could break out at will. The Bonvillion brothers, Randy and Rodney, were two such prisoners.

■ ■ ■

Hailing from Crowley, Louisiana, Randy Bonvillion, 19 and Rodney, 20 were bad, bad men. Springing forth from a childhood that would later be described by their sentencing judge as "tragic" and "brutal," the brothers found themselves behind bars at the MCJ in April of 1980 charged with particularly heinous and sadistic crimes.

The Bonvillions, it was alleged, had kidnapped James Burke, 20, and his fiancée Jackie Hornickel, 21, both of Milwaukee, and taken them on a "nightmare odyssey" through the Upper Keys in early March of 1979. The couple had originally picked the brothers up hitchhiking, during a rainstorm in Cocoa Beach. By the time their abduction was over, Burke had been stomped to death and dumped into a rock pit and Hornickel had been raped at gunpoint, beaten and left for dead. She managed to crawl to the median of U.S. 1 near Tavernier where she was found by a Coast Guardsman and rushed to the hospital.

In October 1979 the Bonvillions were apprehended, along with two runaway girls from California at a bus terminal in New York City. When informed of the charges pending against them in Monroe County, plus the fact that Hornickel was still alive, authorities said the two tried to kill themselves by diving head-first from the upper bunks of their cell, six feet down to the concrete floor below. In addition to their Florida Keys woes, the brothers faced charges in California where they were said to have kidnapped and robbed a wealthy businessman "threatening to pour scalding water on his head if he didn't eat a fistful of narcotics," according to the *Miami Herald*.

■ ■ ■

And so, as the fall of 1980 approached, the Bonvillions, aka the "Moe brothers" sat in the decrepit old Key West jail awaiting

At the time of the crime...

On Jan. 5, 1980 the *Key West Citizen* reported that Edmound K. McIntyre of New Jersey had been arrested after a bizarre armed rampage that saw him kidnap and terrorize two Key West policemen at the Southern Cross Hotel on Duval Street and a Monroe County Sheriff's deputy, a jailer and three tourists at the jailer's home on Josephine Street. Some 75 police officers searched the island for McIntyre, finally cornering him behind a North Roosevelt Boulevard restaurant. He was charged with 28 felonies and sentenced to 90 years in prison for his six-hour spree.

Jailbreak!

Randy Bonvillion

Rodney Bonvillion

trial – or an opportunity to escape.

On the afternoon of Nov. 17 Rodney Bonvillion saw his chance and took it. During a routine shift change of the guards manning the watch tower of the jail's rooftop exercise yard, he and four other inmates scaled the tower, busted out the chain link ceiling and made their way down to freedom. Several sheriff's deputies guarding seized marijuana in trucks outside the building noticed the men, but assumed they were roofers, having been informed earlier that work was being done that day on the building's roof.

Two of the escapees, charged with relatively minor offenses, were caught almost immediately in Bahama Village, the traditionally black area located behind the courthouse complex. But the prime mission of the more than 100-officer manhunt was to capture the 5-foot, 4-inch Bonvillion, described by a sheriff's spokesman as "suicidal, homicidal, schizophrenic, paranoid, very dangerous . . . a danger to society."

Around midnight on the night of the escape Key West police were called to the Days Inn near the by-now roadblocked Cow Key

Bridge, the only route out of town. Some Coast Guardsmen staying at the hotel had encountered a man at the pool who told them he was an oil driller from Louisiana. The Coasties shared some beer with the man, who seemed a little too keen to blend in with their party. Suspecting he might be one of the escapees they had heard about on the radio news, one of them slipped away and called the cops. Officer Bill Henderson arrived on the scene and looking through the window of one of the rooms saw Bonvillion's face reflected in a mirror. The hunted man surrendered peacefully, telling Henderson that he had been staying at the "Bonvillion Motel."

The last two escapees were recaptured in the early morning, one of them discovered in a closet at a Truman Avenue house, the other underneath the bridge to Thompson Island, located at the foot of the Riviera Canal Bridge on South Roosevelt Boulevard.

In the wake of the escape, two jailers quit, knowing their negligence was probably going to get them fired anyway. A third guard, who days earlier had taken two prisoners to a New Town convenience store for a midnight snack – only to see one of them vanish into the night – also handed in his resignation.

Amazingly, two days later, both Bonvillions and four other prisoners overpowered two guards and scrambled to freedom yet again. Besides Rodney Bonvillion, two of the group had been among the escapees from the earlier jailbreak. This time the fugitives didn't get far. Two were discovered hiding behind a stack of cardboard boxes in a stairwell of the courthouse complex while the other four, including both Bonvillions, were found on the building's roof.

The anxious family of Jackie Hornickel, who was to be the prosecution's main witness against the "Moe brothers," could be forgiven for wondering what on earth was going on at the Monroe County Jail.

"Something like that shakes [Jackie] up," Hornickel's mother Dolores told the *Citizen*. "Especially if there was any thought that they might be out long enough to travel."

Jailbreak!

Sadly, Jackie Hornickel's nightmare wasn't over yet.

• • •

On the afternoon of Dec. 29, 1980, an MCJ inmate informed jailers that five of his fellow prisoners had escaped the previous day, including – predictably – Randy Bonvillion.

County authorities immediately set up a roadblock in Marathon, but given the escapees' 17-hour head-start, conceded that they could be in Georgia by now.

"It seems like this year just couldn't go out without something else happening," an exasperated Sheriff William A. Freeman Jr., said.

By New Year's Eve, one of the escapees, James Dillman, was captured in Fort Lauderdale. Meanwhile, with no signs of a forced exit, Freeman's deputies set about finding out who had helped the prisoners escape. The answer came after jail guard Elmer Lee "Joe" Lewis failed a polygraph exam and admitted letting the five out through the jail's laundry room. He had been promised a $2,000 bribe that was supposed to arrive via Western Union, but hadn't. Freeman pronounced himself "disgusted" with this turn of events. Lewis was eventually sentenced to three years in prison for his role in the break-out.

On Jan. 2, 1981, authorities caught a break when Jacksonville, Florida police were tipped off that Randy Bonvillion was hiding out in a trailer in Ortega Farms, a remote rural area outside the city. The trailer was owned by Horace Landry, an old war buddy of Bonvillion's father. Landry told police that Bonvillion had arrived in Jacksonville on New Year's Eve and called him looking for a place to stay. Not realizing that Bonvillion was wanted, Landry agreed and put him up for a couple of days. He had even promised to give him a ride to Georgia, but while out running an errand he saw Bonvillion's "Wanted" poster and realized he was on the lam. Landry then turned him in.

When cornered, Bonvillion offered no resistance as he was taken into custody for the last time.

Neither Bonvillion would ever know freedom again. Randy, in fact, wound up in solitary wearing a straitjacket after he and Dillman slashed their own wrists on Feb. 5, 1981.

By now, Circuit Court Judge Bill Chappell was having a hard time lining up jurors for the Bonvillions' escape trial who hadn't already heard an earful about the brothers' exploits.

"Well, um, they murdered one fellow, raped a girl, and escaped about 14 times," one potential candidate told Chappell. She was excused from the proceedings. Eventually, Chappell bowed to the inevitable and agreed to move the trial to Dade County.

■ ■ ■

Finally, after years of delay, the trial of the Bonvillion brothers began in a Miami courtroom on Jan. 18, 1982. Randy tried to slow things up, complaining of an infected spider bite he said gave him a fever of "101.5" and confined him to a wheelchair, but Circuit Court Judge Herbert Klein was having none of it. The trial was on.

On Jan. 25, the Bonvillions were both found guilty of all counts against them: First-degree murder, attempted murder, sexual battery and two counts each of kidnapping and robbery. Shortly thereafter, Judge Klein followed the jury's recommendation and sentenced the brothers to death for the killing of James Burke. In mid-March, Klein slapped another three life terms – plus 45 years – on both brothers, in case their executions were not carried out. The Moe brothers still faced charges of rape and attempted murder in California and New York State.

Klein's move turned out to be a prescient one. In June of 1983, he himself vacated the death sentences against Randy and Rodney, citing a recent U.S. Supreme Court ruling requiring judges to take defen-

Jailbreak!

dants' background's into consideration before imposing the ultimate punishment.

"The tragedy of their lives may be the reason they did what they did," Klein said in delivering his ruling. "But it is not an excuse."

Now incarcerated in a prison from which there is no escape, the Bonvillions are in the process of becoming history and will spend the rest of their lives as guests of the state of Florida. The "old" Monroe County Jail, from which they repeatedly escaped, already has become history – in part due to its vulnerability to escape demonstrated by desperate and cunning inmates such as the Moe brothers.

By March of 1994, the last of the old jail prisoners had been transferred to a brand new, modern facility on Stock Island where escapes have been rare.

The old jail still exists as storage for county paperwork and parking tickets. But never again will the graffiti-mottled walls of the metal labyrinth echo with the sounds of angry inmates cheering on cellmates such as the Bonvillion brothers as they make a desperate dash for freedom.

BEST SEAT IN THE BIG HOUSE:

Located in the heart of Key West's tourist district, the old County Jail afforded an excellent people-watching vantage point. Prisoners housed in the east side of the building could actually watch Fantasy Fest parades as they snaked down Whitehead Street before the turn onto Duval. Some of the windows on that side of the building even opened and inmates could lower baskets on strings for friends on the ground below to fill with drugs and weapons.

True Crime Stories of Key West and the Florida Keys, Vol. 2

Photo by roboneal.com
The Monroe County Courthouse on Whitehead Street.

Rough Justice

Enraged by a perceived miscarriage of justice, a Conch mob took matters into its own hands. Then all hell broke loose . . . .

Native Key Westers can be an ornery lot – and in the past have not been shy about doling out "bubba justice" if they thought the court system let them down. The community, like others in remote parts of the country, often had to police itself in its early days and that same streak of stubborn self-reliance still lies just below the surface of many an old-school Conch.

Just as dozens of them rose up in 1982 to declare "independence" from the United States, there have been other times when Key Westers have spoken with one angry voice against an unpopular law or judgment.

The spring of 1950 was one of those times.

■ ■ ■

The story began tragically on the evening of May 23, 1950.

Around 9 p.m., Navy Quartermaster Joseph Elmore was driving west on North Roosevelt Boulevard behind a slow-moving Key Island Transit Company bus when he saw a woman plummet from the vehicle to the street. Another witness put the unconscious victim into his car and rushed her to Monroe County Hospital. Doctors did what they could, but at 10:15 p.m., 18-year-old Elena Castillo Harris was pronounced dead by Dr. Herman K. Moore. The cause of death was a fractured skull.

The details of the incident were still sketchy, but the circumstances were described as "highly unusual" in the May 24 edition of the *Key West Citizen*.

The paper reported that the bus driver, Gilberto Blanco Yglesia, 24, had been on his usual route on Stock Island when he spotted his ex-wife, Patricia Yelvington Yglesia, 20, and their two children, Alfred B., 2, and Gilbert B., 4. The Yglesiases, who had recently divorced, got a bite to eat at a Stock Island restaurant with the children, then boarded Gilberto's bus, which was Old Town-bound. Shortly afterwards, however, Gilberto noticed that his air compression belt was broken, disabling the bus's brakes and locking the front door open. He stopped to call his dispatcher to tell him he was bringing the bus back to the garage for repairs, then continued driving towards Old Town.

On the way downtown, Elena Castillo Harris, a young woman with whom Gilberto was said to be "good friends," hailed the bus. She boarded, but moments later, according to what Gilberto and Patricia both told police, she jumped from the vehicle onto the boulevard. The Yglesiases, their children, and Harris were the only riders on the bus at the time.

It was all a little strange and Justice of the Peace Roy Hamelin ordered a coroner's jury to look into the matter the next day. The six-person jury examined the body at the Pritchard Funeral Home and noted that aside from her crushed skull, Harris's only other injuries appeared to be cuts on two of her fingers and slight abrasions on her right arm. Dr. Leonard H. Conly then conducted an autopsy.

The bus was also examined and Gilberto was brought in for questioning. He was then taken to the Monroe County Jail, where he was held on an "open charge of investigation."

His ex was allowed to go free in order to take care of their children.

■ ■ ■

By May 29, 1950, curiosity in the case was at a fever pitch. The much-anticipated inquest into Harris's death proved such a huge

At the time of the crime...

On Aug. 12 1953, "picadillo slinger" Ramon Fernandez of Key West was arrested for assault and battery after heaving a plate of Cuban picadillo, black beans and rice at a waitress at the El Pasaje Restaurant on Truman Avenue. The waitress retaliated by tossing her own plate of black beans at Fernandez. He was sentenced to pay $45 or serve 30 days in the county jail, but later was remanded to custody for not notifying the police of two prior narcotics-related felony convictions.

draw that it was moved from Hamelin's office to the large courtroom at the Monroe County Courthouse in order to accommodate the more than 300 people who showed up to watch. As Gilberto was a fairly recently arrived immigrant from Cuba, Harris the product of an old Key West Cuban/American family and Yelvington an Anglo-American, the Cuban Conch community was taking a keen interest in the outcome of the case.

Gilberto Blanco Yglesia

Several times during the two-hour proceedings, Deputy Sheriff Thomas Dixon called for order and threatened to clear the courtroom as the testimony from the 15 witnesses called and questioned by State Attorney J. Lancelot Lester began to agitate the overflow crowd.

At one point, the dead woman's stepfather, Louis Caraballo, told the court that Elena had received an anonymous, threatening letter on April 7 telling her that the "best thing she could do would be to leave Key West."

He had warned her, Caraballo said, against going through with what he revealed was her proposed marriage – to Gilberto Yglesia.

Shortly after Elena received the letter Caraballo and his wife sent her to Miami to visit an aunt. Before long, Yglesia followed her there and brought her back to the Southernmost City, on the pretext that her mother was sick.

When Patricia Yglesia was called to the stand, she related to the court that she knew Harris by first name and by sight. She said that she had sought out her ex-husband on the day after their divorce because "the children loved to ride the bus with their father." They had eaten at the White Star Café on Stock Island, then headed downtown. Along the way, Elena Harris had hailed the vehicle and Yglesia stopped to pick her up. On the bus, Harris sat down next to the open front door, directly across from where Patricia Yglesia was seated, holding her smallest child, behind the driver's seat.

"Hellos" were exchanged, she said, and then Harris asked her, "Well, are you leaving Key West?" After Patricia Yglesia told her she wasn't, Harris reportedly replied, "Well, why should you?"

Nothing more was said and shortly afterwards Harris suddenly leaped from the bus.

Alarmed, Gilberto brought the damaged vehicle to a stop as soon as he could and then ran "back to the scene of the crime," according to Patricia. Asked by Lester why she had used the word "crime," Patricia replied, "I didn't know what to say, so that is what I said."

Gilberto's testimony was virtually identical to his ex-wife's and Key West Island Transit Company employee Joe Perez confirmed Gilberto's description of the damage to the bus.

Then the bombshell dropped.

A 15-year-old schoolboy named Orfilio Pazos told the court that the bus came to a stop behind him and he walked back to see what had happened. Seeing Patricia Yglesia still sitting on the bus holding her child, he asked her what was going on and was told, "We threw a dog off the bus." (It's not clear from the newspaper accounts whether this exchange between the divorcee and Pazos took place in English or Spanish, but it's entirely possible that Patricia Yglesia was referring to Harris as a female dog – a bitch.)

James Hopkins, another bus driver, then testified that Harris had ridden his bus earlier that evening and had appeared "pale and jumpy," biting her nails and twisting her handkerchief. He said that she had asked him whether Patricia Yglesia would be leaving town. "If she does not, I'll do something about it," he said she told him.

The testimony kept coming.

Walter Knowles told the court that Harris had also asked him whether Gilberto's ex-wife was going to leave town. "You wait and see what will happen if she doesn't," she allegedly told him.

And a Eulalia Tynes, who worked with Harris's mother, said that the dead girl told her "in a few days you will hear of something terrible that is going to happen."

It all set the stage for the next day, when the inquest was supposed to wrap up.

At 2:22 p.m., Dr. Conly took the stand and told the court the results of his autopsy: Harris had died from a fractured skull with edema (swelling of the brain,) causing inter-cranial pressure. State Attorney Lester then asked him if he felt that her injury could have been caused by jumping or falling from a moving vehicle.

"No," Conly replied. "I don't believe it."

■ ■ ■

This response caused an uproar among the capacity crowd in the courtroom.

Conly then asked if Harris had been wearing a hat at the time of her death. Told that she hadn't, he said that in his experience a person falling from "even a rocking chair" would have some sort of marl or dust on them. No traces of either of these substances were found on Harris's body.

The dead girl's head had not touched the pavement, Conly said. She died, he concluded from "a blow from a malleable instrument," such as a blackjack or sandbag that could cause the fatal fracture, without breaking the skin.

Lester thanked the doctor for his time and dismissed him.

At 5:47 p.m. the jury foreman George Schreiber rose and delivered the verdict: Five members of the jury had agreed that Harris had died from falling from the bus. One jurist had dissented.

The verdict created an outraged explosion in the courtroom, with screams of "No!" and "Justice!"

As the *Citizen* wryly put it, "To report that the verdict was an unpopular one would be an understatement of most prodigious proportions."

The angry mob surged forward to the front of the courtroom. Juror Gregorio Rodriguez was grabbed by a man yelling "Let's kill him now." His head was punched and his shirt was ripped by a woman in the mob before he was finally pulled to safety.

Deputy Sheriff Dixon ordered everybody out of the building. His boss, Chief Deputy Sheriff Frank Webber, heard the commotion in his office downstairs and dashed upstairs to help cool the riot and move the crowd to the street, where there was discontented talk of a botched hearing, demands for a new trial – and threats.

"The case was the general topic of conversation in most quarters around the town last night," the *Citizen* reported.

As it turned out, the coroner's jury verdict was not the final word on the matter. By late June, a Grand Jury was empanelled to get to the bottom of Gilberto Yglesia's role in Elena Harris' death.

They never got their chance.

On the afternoon of June 26, 1950, Yglesia and his ex-wife sat on the balcony outside the courthouse where the Grand Jury was preparing to hear the case. Without any warning, Harris's stepfather Louis Caraballo walked up and pumped three bullets into Yglesia, killing him instantly – and causing a stampede of terrified bystanders.

Deputy Sheriff Dixon rushed to the scene with his gun drawn, busted Caraballo and took him downstairs to the Monroe County Jail. He would remain there for the next two years.

Two days later, following a coroner's inquest, Caraballo was charged with first-degree murder at an arraignment held secretly in the courtroom of Justice of the Peace Ira Albury. Also on June 28, Caraballo's feelings – if not his actions – were vindicated when the Grand Jury investigating Harris's death accepted " . . . Dr. H.K. Moore's and Dr. Leonard H. Conly's opinion that Mrs. Elena Castillo Harris met death from a malleable instrument about 8:30 p.m. May 23, 1950. By Majority vote."

Harris' killer was not named, however. And never would be.

Rough Justice

• • •

Following Yglesias's death, the focus of the case shifted to his murderer.

Following an October, 1951 mistrial, Caraballo finally pleaded guilty to second-degree murder in July 1952. As part of a plea arrangement with a prosecution anxious to make the case go away, he was sentenced to 25 years in prison with the possibility of parole after serving eight.

As it happened, he spent 11 years in the clink, returning to Key West in 1963 to work as a laborer for the City of Key West.

The only person to kill a man in cold blood on the Monroe County Courthouse steps died a free man on Aug. 21, 1995, aged 86. He is buried in the Key West City Cemetery.

The question of who murdered Elena Castillo Harris, though, never has been answered – officially.

As Caraballo's attorney Tom Watkins told the court during his 1952 trial, "Only three people know what happened on that bus. And two of them are dead. The third, the wife of Yglesia, has not told what happened . . . ."

Since Patricia Yelvington Yglesia seems to have vanished from Key West, it's unlikely that she ever will. ♀

BRICK (ROUND)HOUSE:

Gilberto Yglesia's employer, the Key Island Transit Company, kept its garage and repair shop in the red brick building at 201 Simonton St. That building, which survived the city's first Great Fire, of 1859, today houses Heatwave Swimwear, Key West Hand Print Fabrics and Peppers of Key West, as well as several second-floor luxury apartments.

Thomas Hayashi

The Mile High Club

Fly Key West offered couples once-in-a-lifetime erotic 'tours.' One day, they flew into the sun . . . .

For better or for worse, Key West is often referred to as a "sexual theme park," tolerant of different kinds of libidinous lifestyles. Not only is the island one of America's iconic gay tourist destinations, but straight men and women regularly come here looking for a little fun in the sun as well. The town's annual Fantasy Fest celebration, held in late October, is a sexually charged diversion for thousands of tourists, many of whom come down with their mates looking for . . . well, other mates!

At any rate, many Key West businesses have sprung up to service these sorts of visitors with everything from lap dances in strip clubs to cool drinks on naked rooftop patios.

There's a lot of money to be made.

One such entrepreneur was pilot Thomas Hayashi, 36, of the Key West Mile High Club.

A native of Texas with more than 5,000 hours of flying experience, Hayashi had come to Key West to seek his fortune in 1990. Along with a friend, he had purchased a 1968 Piper Cherokee and formed the Fly Key West company, offering aerial sightseeing excursions to tourists. Hoping to capitalize on a fad begun in 1916 by Lawrence Sperry – the inventor of the autopilot – Hayashi and his partner converted the back of the Cherokee into a lounge, complete with a bed and video camera. Then they began offering customers the chance to join the "Mile High Club" by having sex high above the ground – and the water.

Under the motto "We fly at 5,280 feet – give or take six inches," the company advertised flights such as "The Quickie," (20 minutes at a 1-mile altitude,) to "The Big Bone Islander," (40 minutes at altitude,) with a premium tacked on for sunset sojourns.

Like other such ventures in California, the trips were an instant hit with the tourists – though many locals cringed. The business, however, seemed legal and so the authorities stayed off of Hayashi's cloud. This would soon change.

On the morning of Aug. 9, 2001, Hayashi said he received a call from a man named "Juan," who was interested in booking a 40-minute reef tour. The man, who spoke broken English with a Hispanic accent, told Hayashi that he and his wife "Rosa" were calling from the Greyhound station just outside the airport. After agreeing on a price of $199 for the excursion, Hayashi picked up the couple and drove them to his plane. Shortly afterwards, the party was airborne.

Ten minutes into the flight, as Hayashi approached "mile high" airspace, the pilot said he encountered some turbulence: The couple was not having sex in the back of his plane. Instead, "Juan" produced a knife, held it to Hayashi's throat and demanded that the pilot plot a course to Cuba.

■ ■ ■

The deteriorating relationship between the American and Cuban governments in the late 1950s had spawned a rash of airplane hijackings between the two countries that peaked in 1969 when some 31 incidents were reported. Many of the hijackers were Cubans fleeing the new government of Fidel Castro, or Cuban-born Americans attempting to return to the island nation in defiance of the U.S.-imposed travel ban. In January of '69, an American Navy deserter hijacked a small plane from Key West to Cuba to avoid being sent to Vietnam.

By 1973, however, the Cuban government had made hijacking a crime, the U.S. had installed metal detectors in its airports and the two countries had signed an extradition accord in Sweden, all of which effectively stemmed the wave of air piracy. But hijacking, like every other crime, never went away entirely. With the travel ban and stringent rules in place on the U.S. side, and the souring economic situation on the communist island, hijackings had picked up again in the 2000s. Hayashi, it

At the time of the crime...

On Oct. 9, 2000 Key West Police Officer Dave Black was summoned to the Bourbon Street Pub on Duval Street after "highly intoxicated" Nancy Lewis was unable to pay her tab. Lewis pulled out a "Shop With Me Barbie" plastic cash register, handed the bartender $20 in "Barbie" money and told him to keep the change. She was arrested and taken to the Monroe County Detention Center, where she told officers "she was going to call 'Stuart Little,' her friend the mouse, to sort out any problems." (*Author's note: Lewis was the* Citizen's *features editor. I ended up with her job!*)

seemed, may have been in the wrong place at the wrong time – and at the wrong altitude.

• • •

Back on the Mile High Club flight, Hayashi's mind was racing.
"There was so much going through my head," Hayashi later told reporter Tom Walker of the *Key West Citizen*. "I thought to myself, 'Tonight I'll be somewhere in Cuba.' But I didn't know where I was going to land, if it was going to be a road somewhere or what."

About 40 miles south of Key West things got really ugly. Hayashi said that his knife-wielding passenger attempted to climb into the co-pilot's seat. Hayashi maneuvered the plane to throw the man off balance, but managed to snap off the aircraft's throttle in the process.

The plane was going down.

Immediately, the pilot radioed the tower at the Key West International Airport and told them he was going to have to ditch. He then gave the two would-be hijackers life jackets and sea belts as the Piper plunged headlong into the 10-foot, whitecap-topped waves below.

Hayashi said he bailed from the plane, but the two hijackers had remained in their seats. The couple had inflated their vests inside the fuselage and might have been unable to fit through the door. Hayashi said he swam back to the plane and tried to open the door, but couldn't.

His eyes stinging from the airplane fuel in the water, Hayashi could only watch as his plane slipped beneath the surface – with both hijackers still belted to their seats. Neither one made it out, Hayashi said. Shortly afterwards, he was spotted by a Coast Guard helicopter crew who dropped him a life raft and hoisted him to safety.

• • •

On Aug. 10, the *Citizen* reported the incident, but Hayashi, speaking through his attorney Marci Rose, was tight-lipped about what had happened.

"He's not talking to anybody," Rose said. "There's an FBI investigation going on and that's the end of it."

But details of the deadly crash began to emerge from Coast Guard spokeswoman Lieutenant Vickie Neblock. "[Hayashi] said [the hijackers] were not moving," as the plane began to sink, she said. The Piper was equipped with an electronic locating device which emits a beacon, but according to Neblock, the Coasties ". . . never even picked up a hit from the ELR," after the plane sank in 3,800 feet of water. Not six hours after the crash, the Coast Guard abandoned its search for the wreckage.

And here the whole story became even more of a barnstormer, as rumors began to swirl around town about what had really happened that day out over the ocean. Some wondered whether there had ever even been passengers aboard Hayashi's plane, or if they had been on board, but died in an unfortunate accident – or an intentional aircraft scuttling.

On Aug. 11, the *Citizen* reported that the FBI still hadn't been able to identify the two passenger/hijackers.

"We have the first names of the victims from the pilot," said Special Agent Judy Orihuela of the bureau's Miami office. "But we're not releasing them at this time."

Hayashi's lawyer was still being extremely tight-lipped about the whole thing.

"[He] was obviously very shaken and hampered by the fact that aviation fuel had gotten into his eyes," Marci Rose said. "He ingested a fair amount of salt water."

Two days later, Hayashi broke his silence in a press release. After thanking all of those who were responsible for his rescue, he got to the meat of the matter.

"Our business ethics have been called into question by some newspapers," he wrote. "Spur of the moment customers are not unusual and whether paying cash or not, the information we had on the customers was normal and our bookkeeping is in order. I would assume people intent on hijacking do not use their real names . . . I had no reason to ask for a photo ID . . . We are not under any investigation that does not relate solely to the facts of this hijacking. The FBI does have some possible leads they are working on."

The next day, Hayashi told the *Citizen's* Walker that he was upset

The Mile High Club

about the rumors making their way around the island and he offered to take a polygraph to clear his name.

"I'll take you out there and you can see for yourself," he said. "See if you would knowingly ditch a plane out there."

Moreover, Hayashi said the whole incident had destroyed his business – but he left open the hope that he would one day fly again.

"I don't have a problem with flying," he said. "I just have a problem flying with people who have knives."

But determining exactly who Hayashi's mysterious passengers had been was proving elusive.

By Aug. 17, the FBI had released composite sketches of the couple to all the local newspapers, but hadn't heard a peep from the public. Nobody, it seemed, had ever heard of the pair before.

And nobody's heard anything about their identities since.

Both the FBI and FAA closed their cases on the matter. Hayashi, his plane and business gone, eventually left Key West.

All that's left of the Key West Mile High Club is an explicit website offering videos made by the frisky couples on its flights; that and a 1968 Piper Cherokee, deep at the bottom of the Straits of Florida, which may – or may not – contain the bodies of two sex plane hijackers named "Juan" and "Rosa."

IN CASE OF EMERGENCY, OPEN WRAPPER:
The Key West Mile High Club advertised their services with folding cardboard matchbooks, each containing a "high altitude" condom.

Courtesy of Monroe County Library

A sketch of Key West, circa 1850.

The First Execution

Key West in the 1830s was a rough-and-tumble town. Some of its residents figured an execution might do the community some good....

The First Execution

The City of Key West has always attracted its share of ne'er-do-wells. While most of the crimes in the earliest days of the settlement involved the relatively harmless drunken escapades of the mostly male, largely seafaring population, there were times when the crimes in question were of such a degree that an example had to be set. Sooner or later, there was going to be a murder. And when it happened, somebody was going to have to pay for such a heinous crime with the most precious possession they owned: Their life.

That time came to the island city in the summer of 1830, just two years after its founding.

Until recently, documentation of the county's first capital case was hard to come by. Thankfully, hard-working Monroe County Library historians Tom and Lynda Hambright have unearthed the diary of a Mr. William Hackley, who chronicled the entire affair for the court and, later on, in his personal journal. By piecing together and deciphering his transcripts, we can present a fascinating glimpse of early justice in old Key West.

■ ■ ■

Key West fisherman Norman Sherwood liked his grog. He liked it so much, in fact, that one blazing hot day, upon which his boat inexplicably remained in port, he decided to while away the hours in an alcoholic fog.

The date was July 5 and Sherwood – perhaps still on a whopping bender from celebrating the nation's independence the day before – wandered into the grog shop of Mr. Abraham Butcher and proceeded to imbibe the foul, rum-based concoction along with several other individuals.

The population of the Southernmost City in those days was a mere 517 souls. That's a pretty cozy number and it meant that those who disliked each other probably saw way too much of their adversaries.

And so it was that on this particular day that Sherwood encountered a fellow grogger known only as Jones – and began to quarrel with him. Incensed, Sherwood put down his glass and went off to his boat. When he returned a short time later, he was carrying a pistol.

Anxious to avoid a shoot-out in his establishment, Butcher told the armed-and-hammered Sherwood that he couldn't come in with the gun. But Sherwood "begged" for more grog to the point that Butcher – acting much like his present-day counterparts in the bar industry might – quickly thought up a solution to the stalemate: He bet Sherwood that he couldn't shoot a flag flying nearby. The ruse seemed to work. Sherwood fired at the flag and then walked away from the scene.

Before long, however, he was back, this time wearing his pistol in a shoulder holster. Butcher would later testify that Sherwood said, "I would look foolish if [Jones] was to shoot me," according to Hackley's journal. Butcher hesitated, but a man named Edward Bassett, who was also present at the grog house, persuaded him to let Sherwood in, figuring that with a few drinks in him the fisherman would be easier to disarm.

He was wrong.

Perhaps emboldened by the booze, Sherwood became increasingly belligerent, advising the pair to back off.

"I don't want to hurt you, Bassett or Butcher," Sherwood said, according to Bassett's later testimony. "But whoever approach me I will shoot."

At this point a friend of Sherwood's named John Wilson, who had been sleeping the grog off in the back of the house, came out and

At the time of the crime...

On Dec. 7, 1831, the *Key West Gazette* reported that some 300 passengers and crew of the recently wrecked ship Maria had taken to drunken rioting in the streets near the port, "in consequence of which the inhabitants at the lower end of the town were prevented from sleeping and were in momentary expectation of having their homes assaulted." U.S. troops kept order until the mob was able to sail on to New Orleans. This was no minor disturbance: At the time the population of Key West was just over 500 people.

The First Execution

confronted his pistol-packing pal. Wilson lunged at the firearm in an attempt to defuse the situation and a scuffle ensued.

Boom!

Sherwood had made good on his word and Wilson dropped to the plank floor, fatally wounded. Bassett then ran to summon Dr. Henry Waterhouse to the scene.

Upon his arrival, Dr. Waterhouse saw that Wilson was already dead. He later testified, as recorded by Hackley, that "On opening the body, found the shot had penetrated into the body, missing the lung and damaging the eighth and fractured the ninth rib."

While the good doctor was examining the body, Sherwood was led back into the grog shop, where he stated that he had no intention to fire at Wilson, but had intended to shoot Jones, who he said had "wronged and abused him." Further, Sherwood told Dr. Waterhouse that "he had no anger against Wilson at the time."

■ ■ ■

On Nov. 9 that same year, Sherwood was arraigned for the murder of John Wilson in the Territorial Court of Judge James Webb in Key West. In marked contrast to the standard strategies employed by today's legal defense teams, who fight tooth and nail to exonerate their clients on any grounds available, Sherwood strangely waived his rights of "preemptory challenge to the full extent allowed by law," Hackley wrote. Late in the afternoon of Nov. 16, the jury brought back a "guilty" verdict against Sherwood. Three days later, on Nov. 19, Judge Webb sentenced Sherwood to hang.

Again, from Hackley, "The judge was so affected that he could hardly get through the sentence and many of the bystanders also were much affected. The prisoner indeed shed a few tears but was not much moved with the hearing of his doom. He walked back to the jail and I am given to understand expressed but little sorrow, saying that he could die only once."

The date of execution had been set for the second Friday in

December and as it approached Sherwood apparently began to change his tune. On Dec. 6 the condemned man ingested a dose of poison that, while not strong enough to kill him, made him deathly ill nonetheless. Sherwood's suicide attempt displeased Hackley, who worried that he might try it again. If he succeeded in this, Hackley wrote, "I would be sorry as the execution of a felon will, I think, have a beneficial effect on this community."

Strangely, for a proponent of the noose, Hackley was actually quite squeamish when the time came to carry out the deed. He was asked to be one of the 30 men guarding Sherwood as he walked from the jail to the execution site, but refused.

"I shall not attend as I am unwilling to see a man hang," he wrote, adding "he is perfectly hardened and ought to suffer the end of a felon." A somewhat schizophrenic stance to be sure.

By Dec. 10, with Sherwood all but recovered from the poison, Hackley closed the book on Sherwood with the following entry in his journal:

"At 10 o'clock a.m., Norman Sherwood was taken from the jail to the gallows erected near the road out from the court house to the west and, in pursuance of the sentence of the law was hung by the neck until he was dead. He said nothing at the gallows and died stubbornly and did not even change color."

The so-far short history of capital cases in Monroe County had begun . . . .

GROG LOG:

Grog is a rum-based drink said to have originated in the British Navy. Following its capture of Jamaica in 1655, a half-pint of rum mixed with a quart of water was part of the Royal Navy's daily ration for more than 200 years. Early on citrus juice was added to the often stagnant water to combat scurvy and lessen its foulness, leading to the labeling of Brits as "limeys."

The First Execution

True Crime Stories of Key West and the Florida Keys, Vol. 2

Courtesy of Monroe County Library
Detective Sergeant Duke Yannacone, right, takes murder suspect Carl Douglas Turner into custody.

On the Down Low

Who would want to kill this friendly pizza man in such a horrifying manner? Veteran Key West cop Duke Yannacone was determined to find out . . . .

There aren't that many closet cases in Key West. This town has always been on the vanguard in accepting its gay population – for the most part, anyway. Tragically, we get our share of visitors here who are in denial of their true orientation. Some of them will do anything to keep their secret.

That's when it becomes a crime story.

■ ■ ■

On the morning of April 25, 1991, Key West police were called to the scene of a gruesome murder. A resident of 4 Aronovitz Lane had returned home from his job at 7:30 a.m. to find his roommate, 27-year-old Hal Leary, butchered in his bedroom. His throat had been slit with such force that Leary had nearly been decapitated. Both his jugular veins had been severed. Red slashes of blood shot across the walls of the bedroom and a trail of bloody footprints led from there to the wide-open back door. Leary's folded body sat in a plastic laundry hamper, naked but for blood-caked socks, which his friends would soon tell police Leary always wore while having sex. The investigation was turned over to Detective Sergeant Duke Yannacone, a cop with 14 years in homicide. Arriving on the scene, Yannacone was disturbed by the violence of the murder. He vowed then and there to find Leary's killer and set to work piecing together what had happened to the affable pizza delivery man.

Leary, who was an "out" gay man, had last been seen around 10 p.m. on Duval Street. Shortly after that, he had called the host of a late-night party in progress to say that he'd be a little late, but would be coming and had some exciting and surprising news. All of Leary's friends knew that he had been single and searching since the previous December and many assumed his announcement concerned his love life.

At the crime scene, Yannacone seemed to be coming to the same conclusion about Leary's final moments.

Leary was a well-liked person with no known enemies. The phone cord in his bedroom had been cut, but there were no signs of forced entry at the house, so the killer was somebody Leary had felt comfortable letting inside. Nothing had been stolen, according to the roommate, ruling out robbery. No drugs were found in Leary's system, so that angle was a dead end too. And next to Leary's bed the cops had found two used condoms. Also, as the bloody footprints showed, the killer had been barefoot. Perhaps he had been completely naked at the time of the killing?

As crime scene detectives cut up sections of the bloody floor with a circular saw, a mysterious figure watched the proceedings from the corner of the street. Little did the probers know that their work was being monitored by the man who had murdered Hal Leary.

■ ■ ■

Sifting through the evidence later on, Yannacone thought he knew what had happened: Leary's throat had been cut as he lay on the bed and the killer had quickly exited the room. Leary had gotten out of bed and tried to open the door, but the murderer held it tightly closed until he heard Leary fall heavily into the laundry hamper.

The news of the Leary murder ran on page one of the *Key West Citizen* on April 26.

Very quickly Yannacone began hearing from numerous locals, including many of Leary's friends. They all told the same story. Leary had been seen around town with a man none of them knew. It soon became clear that they were all talking about the same person. He was tall, over six feet, in his mid-twenties with dark hair. They also said he wasn't your typical gay bar customer, looking more like a biker-type, with a "Harley" eagle tattoo. He wasn't real friendly, they all said, and looked a little uncomfortable hanging out with the regulars at the bars.

From the descriptions provided to him Yannacone had a police artist draw up a composite sketch. He showed the sketch to a bartender at the last establishment where Leary had been seen hanging out with his mystery man. The barkeep told Yannacone the sketch was a good likeness and mentioned that he overheard the man say that he was from Fort Myers on Florida's Gulf Coast.

At the time of the crime...

On Oct. 1, 1991 Key Wester Nicholas Maus was arrested for throwing a six-foot rattlesnake at his girlfriend after catching her in bed with another man. The woman told police that Maus first used the snake to chase his romantic rival out of their Duck Avenue apartment, then turned on her and her daughter with the reptile. The women responded by throwing the snake back at him. No snake bites were reported and the rattler was unharmed. Maus was charged with domestic battery and possession of a dangerous animal without a permit.

A couple of days later the sketch ran in the *Citizen*. That morning, the phone in Yannacone's office rang and a woman who claimed to be a waitress at a local restaurant told the sleuth that she had been living with the man in the sketch. His name was Roger Hunter, she said, and he had come to Key West from Fort Myers. She said that he had left town that very morning in the car he had been driving when she met him, a black '87 Nissan.

Mere hours later, Yannacone and his parter, Detective Sergeant Gary Armstrong, were trudging through numerous Fort Myers-area bars showing the sketch around to clients at places frequented by bikers – and gays. Several people recognized the man and told Yannacone and Armstrong that his real name was Jimmy Roger Hunter and that he was kind of a weird loner that nobody really knew all that well.

More than once the two cops were told that Hunter seemed to like men more than women. He often lived with a girl, but prowled the bars alone at night seeking clandestine sex with other men.

• • •

Back in Key West, the cops searched through a computer database and found that Hunter had pawned some power tools and a shotgun in Key West just days before Leary's murder. Now Yannacone and Armstrong had a photo ID and thumb print to use on a nationwide arrest/conviction search. They discovered that Hunter was wanted in California for violating probation. Yannacone now had everything he needed to start the process of arresting his suspect. He issued an arrest warrant for Hunter for possession of a firearm, which is illegal for convicted felons, and asked for and received a request for bail of $150,000.

Just days after the warrant went out over the national crime database, Yannacone began receiving calls from law enforcement agencies all over the country, who had men named Jimmy Roger Hunter in custody. But each time, the men had nothing in common with the Key West killer but the name. One day, after asking a caller if the man in custody was 6-foot-2 and had an eagle tattoo, Yannacone received a surprising answer. "No, no, you don't understand," said the caller, an Alabama policeman, "We have the real Jimmy Roger Hunter."

It turned out that a Jimmy Roger Hunter of Alexander City, Alabama had had his ID stolen two years earlier by a tall man from Tennessee. Suddenly Yannacone felt the case slipping away from him. If Jimmy Roger Hunter hadn't killed Hal Leary, who had?

Then Yannacone caught a break. He got a hit on the black Nissan the killer had been driving. It had been stolen from a woman in Tennessee who claimed her ex-boyfriend Carl Douglas Turner had taken the car without her permission.

Turner's alias? Jimmy Roger Hunter.

The woman described her ex as a tall man, over six feet, and suddenly Yannacone was back in the game. He ran Carl Turner's name though the database and discovered a lengthy rap sheet including charges of robbery and car theft.

Convinced now of Turner's true identity, Yannacone began interviewing the man's relatives and associates and waited for that last break he needed to find and arrest Carl Douglas Turner.

■ ■ ■

As it happened Turner hadn't left the state. Penniless and on the run, he had been living off the proceeds of whatever robberies he was able to commit, and doing his best to keep a low profile. That is, until 9/11/91. Early in the morning that day, there was an altercation at a homeless shelter in Pensacola that brought the cops there to straighten things out. Not long after they left a tall young man whispered to his bunkmate, "Whew! It's a good thing they didn't run a check on my car." He motioned to a green Oldsmobile parked outside. "It's stolen."

The bunkmate immediately called the police, who quickly returned to the shelter. "Who's driving that Olds?" they asked the hushed dormitory.

"I am" came the response.

And with that, "Jimmy Roger Hunter" was taken into custody.

Shortly after arresting the man, the Pensacola cops called Yannacone's Key West home. "We've picked up a Jimmy Roger Hunter and I see he's wanted in Key West," the officer told Yannacone.

"How tall is he?" came Yannacone's response.

"Six-foot-three."

"Does he have a tattoo?" Sure enough he did. Yannacone jumped out of bed and booked a 5 a.m. flight to Pensacola. Shortly after his arrival, Yannacone was led into an interrogation room where he came face-to-face with his

On the Down Low

adversary. Within 15 minutes Turner had confessed to killing Hal Leary.

At first Turner claimed that the two had been smoking crack at Leary's house. He had become disgusted with Leary's sexual advances towards him and had "just lost it," and sliced his throat with a buck knife.

Knowing no drugs had been found in Leary's bloodstream, and aware of Turner's unease with his sexuality, Yannacone gently suggested to Turner that Turner tell him the whole story.

Very quickly, Turner 'fessed up and told the detective what he already had surmised: Turner had met Leary at a bar and returned home with him to have sex. Two days later, the pair met up again and went back to Leary's place for a repeat performance. In the afterglow, Leary confessed to Turner that he felt like he was falling in love with him. This got to Turner, who was worried about anybody finding out his true orientation.

Several days later, on the night he killed Leary, Turner said the two had just finished having sex at Leary's house when the pizza man suggested to Turner that he accompany him to the party he was planning on attending that evening. He had been telling all his friends about his new "Mr. Right," he said, and wanted to show him off.

Instead, Turner grabbed a buck knife that Leary kept on his nightstand and nearly beheaded him with it.

He then threw on some of Leary's clothes and walked to a nearby beach where he cleaned himself in the surf. This done, he walked over to his girlfriend's house and acted as if nothing had happened. The next day, he wandered by the crime scene to watch the cops processing it.

Turner showed no remorse during his confession and remained unrepentant as he was sentenced to life-plus 40 years in prison.

He remains incarcerated at the Florida Correctional Institution – and a prisoner of his own repressed sexuality. ▲

A BUILDING BUILT ON GUILT:

The Domino's Pizza location on Truman Avenue where Hal Leary worked once housed the Ringside Billiards parlor, known for its illegal back-room gambling. It was the scene of an infamous holdup by corrupt Key West policeman Sam Cagnina on Aug. 7, 1960. Today an adult video store occupies the space.

True Crime Stories of Key West and the Florida Keys, Vol. 2

Photo courtesy of Monroe County Library

The *U.S.S. Stribling* **at Oran, North Africa, in 1954.**

He Was Expendable

*U.S.S. Stribling was the flagship
of one of America's foremost military leaders.
In Key West she became the scene
of a horrifying crime . . . .*

He Was Expendable

Federal murder trials in Monroe County are extremely rare: To date, there have only been two, and only one of those resulted in a guilty verdict. When such trials do occur they are usually accompanied by a national media circus, with reporters hanging on every detail of the proceedings.

This is the somewhat mysterious tale of a single incidence of murder aboard a locally based Navy vessel, the subsequent investigation, and the outcome of what became the first ever federal murder trial in Key West.

■ ■ ■

On the morning of July 25, 1946 the 250 crew members of the destroyer *U.S.S. Stribling DD-867* were summoned on deck for a roll call. Not long afterwards, at a second muster, they were informed that a vicious murderer likely stood amongst them.

Around 9:15 a.m., that day, the bloodied body of Seaman Second Class Benjamin LeRoy Long Hobbs, 19, was found by a shipmate under a canvas tarp in gun tub 43. Hobbs, whose absence at the first muster had sparked a shipwide search, was clad only in his undershorts, which had been partly ripped from his body. The ship's skipper had inspected the men during the musters and demanded that each account for their whereabouts during the night.

Before long a suspect had emerged, though the Navy kept this info a secret for some time. He was Third Class Navy Cook David Joseph Watson, an "extremely dark," "colored" "negro," as the press would later take great pains to point out. The authorities however pronounced themselves "baffled" by the case. The missing piece of the puzzle – and it was a big one – was a motive. It would take two years and as many trials to learn exactly what happened to Hobbs that night and to bring his killer to justice.

■ ■ ■

At nearly 400 feet in length, displacing 2,250 tons and bristling with state-of-the-art weaponry and surveillance equipment, *Stribling* was an imposing sight at the Key West Naval Base. Described by one of her creators as "more of a light cruiser" than a destroyer, this leviathan had been launched at New York City a year earlier under the command of the celebrated and controversial Commander John C. Bulkeley. Just 34 years old, Bulkeley was already considered a living legend for his daring rescue of General Douglas MacArthur from the Philippines in 1942, an act that earned him the Congressional Medal of Honor. Further recognition of his exploits came in the 1945 film "They Were Expendable," based on Bulkeley's life and starring John Wayne and Robert Montgomery.

"She's a real fighting ship," a proud Bulkeley told the *Staten Island Advance* newspaper on Sept. 6, 1945.

Following Stribling's "shakedown" cruise to the U.S. Naval Station at Guantanamo Bay, Cuba (to iron out any mechanical bugs,) she made for Key West, where she was assigned to be the flagship of the top-secret Fleet Sonar School. It was in this capacity that the vessel, by now under the charge of Commander Phillip W. Mothersill, became the backdrop for the murder investigation.

Two days after the discovery of Hobbs' body in the 40-millimeter gun tub, the authorities were still saying little, drawing a "heavy curtain of mystery around the strange death," according to the *Miami Herald*. It was rumored that Hobbs had been bludgeoned and strangled, but the Navy refused to confirm or deny this. The news blackout, the *Herald* reporters wrote, was "reminiscent of the Navy in wartime." Members of the press were allowed onto the base, but the ship, now grounded indefinitely, was off-limits. Even garbage being removed from *Stribling*

At the time of the crime...

In 1946, the Key West Civil Service Board suspended Patrolman Frank Jolly for three days for "promiscuous use of a firearm" after Jolly "fired his pistol into the air . . . in pursuit of a taxi driver," according to the *Key West Citizen*.

was being checked for evidence.

By July 29, 1946, the *Key West Citizen* was reporting that Watson, the confined prime suspect, had already attempted suicide three times. He had hanged himself with his tie, slammed his head against the wall of his cell and "hacked" at his tongue with his teeth, all the while pleading his innocence.

Hobbs' body, according to the *Citizen*, was "not allowed to be viewed by friends who were told the sight was way too grueling."

On July 30 the paper stated that a hangman's noose had been discovered in Watson's possession. That day the ship's crew had been ordered to report to the stations they had manned at the time the murder occurred, as blimps hung over *Stribling* snapping photographs of the proceedings.

Meanwhile, Navy divers scoured the bottom of the harbor in the area around the destroyer for the murder weapon. At one point the frogmen discovered a hammer wrapped in a rag, but upon closer examination, investigators later conceded that the tool probably had nothing to do with the case.

Two days later, an official autopsy revealed that Hobbs had died of slow strangulation around 3:15 a.m., after being struck twice on the head with a blunt instrument.

Following the release of the coroner's report, the murdered teen's body "began its sad journey home . . . to Marion, N.C. for burial," the *Citizen* reported. The same article contained a sensational suggestion: "Unofficial sources claim sex perversion entered into the killing."

Suddenly, FBI investigators could see a motive taking shape.

■ ■ ■

By Aug. 2, with Watson in custody and the case against him beginning to gel, the Navy released 16 men to separation centers, as previously scheduled, for demobilization from the armed forces. Hobbs was to have been among them. In solidarity, Hobbs' shipmates took up a collection for his widowed mother, who had been looking forward to her son's return to their rural North Carolina farm.

At last, on Aug. 9, both the *Citizen* and *Herald* reported that Watson, finally, had confessed to the murder. The cook said that he had returned to *Stribling* from shore leave on the night of the murder and due to the summer heat decided to sleep on deck. Waking up in the wee hours, he noticed Hobbs sleeping in gun tub 43. Watson attempted to "assault" Hobbs, according to Chief Joseph Thornton of the FBI, and panicked when the young man awoke and fought back. Looking around for a weapon, Watson said he grabbed a wrench and struck Hobbs in the back of the head several times. He then used the cord from a canvas tarpaulin as a garrote to finish him off.

Though the motive had been hinted at, authorities still could find no real reason for Watson to kill Hobbs. To get to the bottom of the mystery, Watson was transferred to Naval Air Station Jacksonville on Aug. 22 for a psychiatric examination. The results would determine whether the suspect, described by people around him as highly intelligent, but "warped" and "sexually abnormal," would face a Navy court martial or a murder trial in civilian courts. Just over a month later, on Sept. 28, 1946, the answer came back: A grand jury in Jacksonville, acting on the recommendations of the Navy shrinks, indicted Watson for first-degree murder. Trial was to take place Nov. 4, 1946, before U.S. District Court Judge John W. Holland at the federal courthouse in Key West. Prosecutors announced their intention to seek the death penalty.

• • •

On day one of the first federal murder trial in Key West history, Watson pleaded "not guilty," with his court-appointed lawyer John G. Sawyer at his side and his mother, Inez Watson, of Norfolk, Virginia also present. The trial was a sensational event for the small town, with a jury pool drawn from eight Florida counties, a heavy press contingent and elements of sex, violence and racism thrown in. The presence of Watson's devoted mother added an element of poignancy to the proceedings.

The next day it was revealed that Watson, who was on a 24-hour suicide watch, had somehow managed to obtain two razor blades and a heavy steel "club like" instrument, identified as part of the lock mechanism from a cell door, while on the mainland.

"Only a . . . restraining belt prevented a possible attack on either one of the two of us who brought Watson down here," Miami Deputy U.S. Marshal Myrtland Cates told the *Citizen*.

On Nov. 7 the paper reported that government prosecutor Hayford O. Enwall asked a pair of medical examiners "whether sodomy had been committed." One of the examiners "'could not state' what had occurred but his testimony strongly indicated such a possibility," the *Citizen* said.

The next day witnesses described seeing Watson carry his bedding into gun tub 45, adjacent to Hobbs' on the night in question. Also, an FBI investigator told the court that he had discovered drops of blood in both gun tubs and a trail of blood between the two.

But the most damning testimony of all wouldn't be admitted into evidence. Steward Harry C. White, Watson's superior, related that Watson had been at least an hour and a half late for his 5 a.m. shift on the morning of July 25. Further, when the crew was asked who had slept on deck during the night Watson had remained silent, though he later went over to the officer in charge of the muster and talked to him for a few minutes. Watson then followed the superior on deck. When he returned, a "jittery" Watson asked White "What would a man get if he killed another in the Navy?"

"OBJECTION!" defense lawyer Sawyer yelled. A body had just been discovered, he pointed out, and it was natural that any of the sailors might have been having similar thoughts. Moreover, Sawyer told Judge Holland, with the murderer still at large the whole crew had been jittery that morning. Holland agreed and threw out the testimony.

Sawyer soon scored a second coup when Holland agreed not to allow Watson's written confession to be admitted as evidence, as the burly cook had not been advised of his constitutional rights at the time it was obtained.

The government struck back when prosecutor Enwall put FBI

agent Wallace B. Foarde on the stand to relate a conversation he had overheard while standing in the same room as Watson and his mother.

The defendant, according to Foarde, told his mother that he had gone "over towards the person lying face down and he started to bother with him like he was a woman. . . . the person [Hobbs] woke up and called him by name and said 'Watson, I am going to report you to the executive officer in the morning.'" At that point Watson told his mother he hit Hobbs over the head with the wrench and then strangled him to death with the tarpaulin cord. Since the statement had been made freely in the presence of Foarde, Holland allowed it to be admitted into evidence as the prosecution's strongest weapon yet against Watson. In addition, when court resumed two days later, Holland decided that, in light of Foarde's testimony, Watson's written confession could be read in court after all. The details in the statement, according to the *Citizen*, were "too revolting for publication."

The *Herald*, however, had no such scruples about the content. After killing Hobbs, Watson wrote, "I left him and went back to where I was sleeping. A short time later I returned. The body was still warm. I thought he was unconscious. It was then I committed a sexual act."

By the end of the day the prosecution rested its case.

The next day, following a quick tour of the crime scene by the judge, jury and defense and prosecution teams, defense attorney Sawyer also called it quits without putting a single witness on the stand. Both sides were to make their closing statements the next day.

Watson, for his part, was reported to have broke down and cried as he left the courtroom.

During his summation, prosecutor Enwell described Watson's alleged deed as "savage, barbaric, wicked" and "evil." He also pointed out that since the wrench Watson confessed to having used to kill Hobbs was stored in a place "not readily accessible" to the crime scene, the killing had been a premeditated act. "Watson intended to destroy his victim if he would not consent to his unnatural sex desires," he told the court.

Following Sawyer's brief summation, the case was handed off to

He Was Expendable

the jury. By 9:45 the next morning, the verdict was in: Guilty. With a mandatory death sentence. The jury had decided upon Watson's guilt the night before, but a lone holdout, Ezekiel Q. Rodgers of Miami Beach, had favored a life sentence for Watson. The *Citizen* called it "interesting" that a former resident of Georgia, such as Rodgers, would take such a position. Sawyer too, seemed surprised. During his summation he had said he didn't believe people from Georgia "would render a fair verdict because of the racial question involved." Before the dismissal of the court, Sawyer made clear his intention to appeal the sentence and seek a new trial for Watson.

• • •

By January of the next year, Sawyer had gotten his wish. Judge Holland set aside the original verdict and granted a new trial for Watson, who was facing imminent execution. The defense argued that Watson had been insane at the time of the killing and that the jury had not been instructed on the proper meaning of "premeditated."

The victory, however, proved to be a short-lived one for the defense. On Aug. 7, 1947, Watson was again found guilty of first-degree murder. On Aug. 21, Holland denied a defense motion for a new, third trial and Watson was sentenced to die in the electric chair at Raiford State Penitentiary, in the town of Starke, in north-central Florida.

On Sept. 15, 1947, Watson kept his date with destiny following a brief conversation with his mother.

His final words?

Don't ask. I won't tell . . . .

RETURN ENGAGEMENT:
During David Joseph Watson's second trial in Key West, he was prosecuted by U.S. Attorney Herbert S. Phillips. The lawyer was known to Key Westers as the man who successfully prosecuted Fred Ewert, the last man to be executed in Monroe County, in 1904.

Photo courtesy of Monroe County Library
Coast Guardsmen escort crew from the *Bahama Mama* back to the cutter *Half Moon* on Jan. 11, 1967.

Deadliest Catch

With threats and accusations flying around the fishing docks, it was only a matter of time before this crawfish turf war escalated. Nobody dreamed how far it would go . . . .

What's not to like about Florida Keys seafood?

From stone crab claws to snapper, grouper and Key West pink shrimp, this place is blessed with the bounty of the sea. It's big business too. Each year, Monroe County's fishing industry employs thousands of workers who generate tens of millions of dollars in revenue for the area economy and seafood for local tables.

It can be a cutthroat business though, and many fishermen aren't shy about asserting their rights to fish where they see fit. Lobstering in particular lends itself to territorial disputes, as traps are stationary and the harvest is so valuable. It's understood that about the worst act a lobster fisherman can commit is to pilfer from – or cut – another man's traps and many lobster boats carry small arms to defend their catches against such practices. When tempers flare up between armed men at sea – it can be hell.

■ ■ ■

It was around 8 a.m. on the chilly day of Jan. 11, 1967 when the U.S. Coast Guard received a frantic distress call. An unidentified vessel was being fired upon by another boat in the area around the Cay Sal Bank, located about 70 miles southeast of Marathon, in Bahamian waters.

Though Florida spiny lobsters, or crawfish, as they are sometimes called, have always been plentiful in the waters around the Keys, many fishermen venture further offshore in search of bigger catches. The remote Cay Sal Bank is an ideal spot for a huge payoff.

Not knowing what to expect, three Coast Guard cutters and four aircraft responded to the desperate call for help.

Upon their arrival, crewmen from the cutters encountered a number of Keys-based fishing boats floating silently in the surf. But the tranquility of the scene was deceptive. Before the Coast Guard's arrival the fishermen had engaged in a 90-minute shootout over trapping rights in the rich lobstering grounds.

A boarding party from the 311-foot cutter *Half Moon* armed with .45 caliber pistols and M-16 rifles and burst onto the deck of the 44-foot *Bahama Mama* out of Marathon. The lobster boat was so riddled with bullets, one observer later recalled, that it looked like "Swiss cheese." On the deck of the *Mama*, the Coasties rushed to the aid of the vessel's skipper, Capt. William Branthoover, who was bleeding from bullet wounds to his right arm and leg. A second, armed, but unharmed crewmember was also detained.

Minutes later, another USCG boarding team seized a similar lobstering boat, the *Trojan*, out of Stock Island and detained its heavily armed three-man crew, including Captain Ray Vanyo.

Two other lobster boats apparently involved in the fray — the *Bunky III* and *Billy J* — both out of Marathon, were secured, with the latter offering up a gruesome and unwanted surprise: The boat's mate, Vern Austin, lay dead on the deck, his heart pierced by a .303 slug. As the wounded Branthoover was airlifted to a Miami hospital, the Coasties grimly set about steering the battle-scarred boats back to Marathon. The now-disarmed fishing crews and the body of Vern Austin were safely secured aboard the Coast Guard vessels. Over on the *Billy J*, cold and wet Coast Guard Senior Chief Quartermaster Richard Brooks quietly slipped on the dead mate's shirt to keep warm in the face of an oncoming Nor'easter.

So far, the whole incident was a bit of a mystery to the authorities. What exactly had happened out on the Bank? And who, or what, was to blame?

■ ■ ■

As soon as one group of the beleaguered fishermen hit the dock in Marathon they were whisked away by the FBI for interrogation, leaving a pack of newspaper reporters and photographers to wait for their first

At the time of the crime...

On Jan. 3, 1967 the *Key West Citizen* reported that its own classified advertising manager Jim Hill had been shot dead during an argument over a woman. The suspect, Navy Yeoman Gary Preble was charged with first-degree murder, but was acquitted in February of 1968.

Deadliest Catch

glance of the shot-up lobster boats and any scraps of information they could find.

The tattered vessels finally arrived in the wee hours of Jan. 12, escorted by the *Half Moon*. The remaining fishermen, including Ray Vanyo, were led from the cutter and brought to join their colleagues, as the FBI, Coast Guard and Monroe County Sheriff's Office tried to connect the dots in the case.

Later that day, Vanyo was formally charged with "murder on the open seas" and brought to the Monroe County Jail in Key West to await his trial on a no-bond hold.

None of the other fishermen were charged for their roles in the deadly melee, which was now beginning to make some sort of sense to the authorities: The skippers of the *Bahama Mama*, *Billy J* and *Bunky III* were all related by blood, though the FBI stated that the *Bunky* hadn't actually been involved in the shooting. Clearly this was a turf war at sea, with Vanyo and his crew on one side and the rest of the boats on the other.

The body of Vern Austin was then transported to Key West for his funeral. It had been just the second lobster fishing trip for the now deceased father of six.

■ ■ ■

At Vanyo's Jan. 29 hearing before U.S. Commissioner William Albury in Key West, details began to emerge about the situation leading up to the shootout.

Robert McCulley, a crewman from the *Bunky III* stated that "Branthoover 'didn't want anyone to fish in that area,'" the *Miami Herald* reported. "He wanted it for the Miller family." Vanyo had been fishing "about a mile from there," he said.

Another lobsterman, Erwin Michalak out of Stock Island, concurred with McCulley stating that "Branthoover had blocked out a 27-mile by 8-mile area where he said 'no traps within that part . . . Branthoover said he would cut our traps away . . . Ray (Vanyo) said he would stay away.'"

Branthoover's father-in-law John Miller, captain of the *Billy J*, admitted there had been heated arguments at the fishing docks and on the

Photo courtesy of Monroe County Library

The *Bunky J* and *Billy III* in the aftermath of the Jan. 11, 1967 lobster war at Cay Sal Bank.

water between his kin and Vanyo over fishing at Cay Sal, but denied his family ever trying to monopolize the area. They were just trying to protect their own rights, he said.

"Vanyo 'was setting his traps within 20 feet of mine . . . I told him they were too close . . . get them out or we'll cut them away.'"

On the morning of Jan.11, Miller had been fishing about 250 feet from Vanyo, he said, "when I heard a lot of shooting . . . I turned and headed southwest . . . there was a swarm of bullets coming at me.

"Austin never fired a shot," he continued. "When I turned around I saw him falling down." Miller then picked up his own gun and returned fire. "If I could have hit someone, I would."

For his part, defense attorney Carr did his best to have the court knock the charge against his client down to manslaughter, in view of the circumstances.

"The Branthoover-Miller clan sticks together," Carr said. "Vanyo's traps were willfully and intentionally cut by the clan."

But Commissioner Albury refused to consider any charge less than murder. The confrontation had been brewing for days and was therefore pre-meditated. Furthermore, the bullet that killed Austin had been purchased by Vanyo 24 hours before the shootout.

In the end, Vanyo was indicted for the murder of Austin, a man he'd never met.

Again, bail was denied.

• • •

By the time the proceedings got underway in late September, 1967, Vanyo's crewmen, George Broome and Nevin Fitz, were on trial with him – for their lives. This rare, juried federal murder case would take place in the courtroom of U.S. Judge Ted Cabot at the federal building in Key West.

The defense strategy was clear: Show that the Branthoover-Miller family had intimidated and threatened rival fishermen, destroying their property and attempting to assert their control over Cay Sal. Carr also sought to demonstrate that in the midst of the chaotic gun battle none of the parties blazing away could possibly have known where all their bullets hit and that Austin had simply gotten caught in the crossfire and killed.

Branthoover, first on the stand, pretty much admitted this, stating that he "could not be sure where his bullets struck," the *Key West Citizen* reported on Sept. 28. The *Bahama Mama* skipper, under cross examination by Carr, also admitted that his initial statement to the FBI "had some contradictions in it."

Again he was accused by Carr of trying to keep non-family members from fishing the area, of misleading Vanyo with false weather reports and of warning both Vanyo and fellow lobster boat captain Erwin Michalak that he'd cut their traps if they were dropped too close to his.

Finally, Branthoover admitted that just prior to the shooting he'd cut away some of Vanyo's traps, which was the "last straw" for his already steamed rival boat captain. It was then that Vanyo opened fire on the *Bahama Mama*. Like two prize fighters, the boats circled each other, blasting away, as the *Billy J* floated nearby. Eventually, shots fired from the *Trojan* struck the engine of the *Mama*, bringing her to a stop.

When two bullets hit Branthoover, he ordered his mate to wave a white "flag," he said. Vanyo then boarded the boat and stuck a .38 caliber pistol under his chin, snarling "you son of a bitch, I ought to kill you."

Branthoover claimed that he responded with "shake hands, you win," and "we'll fish together from now on."

• • •

Day two of the trial held more surprises. It was revealed that *Trojan* crewman Nevin Fitz had told the FBI shortly after the shooting that Vanyo had fired the first shot. Fitz also claimed that the crew of the *Billy J* had fired at the *Trojan* and that he had shot back.

After that, with bullets buzzing around like angry hornets, it was nearly impossible to tell who was shooting at what.

As the trial continued, government witness Leon Miller, captain of the *Bunky III*, told the court that Vanyo had laid his lobster traps across existing traps lines in the area, telling the other boat captains that he'd "drop them anywhere he wanted." The *Trojan* then left the area and came back two days to harvest the lobster from the traps. Only this time the boat was "loaded for bear" with plenty of guns and ammunition. The shooting started shortly thereafter.

On Oct. 4, the defense called a surprise witness, Big Pine Key fisherman Craig Pontin, who claimed that some time before the incident involving Vanyo, Branthoover had threatened to disable his traps and shoot out his engine if he fished the Cay Sal Bank. Another defense witness, Robert McCulley also of the *Bunky III*, stated that Branthoover threatened to "put a bullet" in him following his previous testimony at the January hearing.

It was just these kinds of threats that had compelled the three crewmembers of the *Trojan* to arm themselves, Carr told the jury.

"A warning shot was fired across the bow (of the *Bahama Mama*) to advise them they could not destroy property . . . this was sheer piracy on the high seas . . . we believe they were justified in protecting their rights."

In closing, the government argued that even if Austin had been killed in the crossfire by a shot from the *Bahama Mama*, it was the fault of Vanyo, who had fired the first shot.

Defense attorney Carr stressed the threats that had been made against rival fishermen by members of Branthoover's family, saying that the *Trojan* crewmembers were only trying to earn a living.

"I wasn't shooting to kill anyone," Vanyo said. "I was concerned with our safety and the protection of my boat and rights."

• • •

The very next day the 12-person jury took just three and a half hours to render its verdict: All three men were found not guilty of all charges and released from custody, free to resume fishing, presumably, wherever they liked.

With that somewhat anti-climactic denouement, the Cay Sal Bank lobster war of 1967 was over. Its memory haunts Keys fishermen, however, as an example of what can happen when greed trumps common sense and respect in the quest for the almighty dollar.

It was a lesson lost on Vanyo, however. After the Bahamas gained full independence from Britain in June of 1973, Keys lobstermen could no longer fish the Cay Sal Bank and many turned elsewhere for work. In December of 1985 Vanyo, his son Ray Jr. and two other men were convicted of masterminding a local pot smuggling ring. The former lobsterman, who beat a murder rap, was sentenced to 14 years – with no chance of parole – over square grouper, as pot bales are often referred to in the Keys. ♀

BAHAMA TRAUMA:

Numerous instances of American fishermen running into trouble in Bahamian waters have been recorded. One November day in 1962 two University of Miami students and their experienced skipper disappeared during a lobster fishing trip near South Riding Rock Island. Their boat Revenge was discovered floating upside down in the water with what appeared to be bullet holes in its hull. There were no rocks or reefs in the area, and the boat's food and water supply was untouched. A congressional investigation was launched but no trace of the missing men was ever discovered.

True Crime Stories of Key West and the Florida Keys, Vol. 2

Photo courtesy of Monroe County Library

At left, The Russell House hotel on Duval Street.

The Castanon/Reyes Affair

Spanish loyalist Don Gonzalo Castanon came to Key West from Cuba itching for a fight with revolutionary Juan Maria Reyes. He got more than he bargained for . . . .

The Castanon/Reyes Affair

The ties that bind Key Westers and Cubans are so numerous that multitudes of books have been written about them. From the 1850s onward, Key West served as a launch pad for guerrilla actions against Cuba when that country was a Spanish colony — to the point that Cuban liberation icon Jose Marti called Key West "The cradle of Cuban independence." As the Cuban struggle against the Spanish authorities intensified in the late 1800s, many Cuban businessmen and others sympathetic to the cause of Cuban freedom were forced to seek refuge in the Southernmost City of the United States, less than 100 miles from Havana. They built cigar factories and community meeting places such as the San Carlos Institute on Duval Street and left an indelible imprint on the culture of this small island.

Just as Miami has become the stronghold of Cuban exiles fleeing the Castro regime since 1959, Key West was once the citadel of pro-independence Cubans who gathered here to plot revolution against Spain in the years leading up to the Spanish American War in 1898.

Among the loudest of these voices calling for Cuban independence was Juan Maria Reyes, editor of the influential Key West newspaper *El Republicano*. In counterpoint to revolutionaries like Reyes were Spanish loyalists such as Don Gonzalo Castanon, editor of the Havana-based *La Voz de Cuba*.

There was clearly no accommodation possible between such divergent views, as became apparent early in 1870, when a public row between the two men escalated into an incident that would eventually impact the course of Cuban history.

As with many quarrels, it's difficult to know who fired the first rhetorical shot, but according to the spring 2001 *Florida Keys Sea Heritage Journal*, it's thought that the ill-feeling between the two slowly built over time, culminating in an editorial attack by Castanon in *La Voz de Cuba*, directed at Reyes. According to the *Journal*, Reyes responded that Castanon "only used such language because he knew that Reyes could not go to Havana."

The stage was set for a confrontation between the two, and how it would turn out was anybody's guess.

■ ■ ■

On Jan. 21, 1870, Castanon's newspaper published his response to Reyes' assertion: An offer to come to Key West to fight a duel of honor to settle the matter.

Not receiving an answer, Castanon did not hesitate to put his words into action. On the morning of Jan. 29, 1870, he arrived in Key West along with six other Spaniards aboard the steamer *Alliance*. Though the town was enemy territory, politically speaking, *El Republicano* reported that "The Cuban population received them without a demonstration or ill will, without shouting, like accomplished gentlemen do in their own home, accepting all [the] insults that for more than one year, they [had] been suffering from this bloodthirsty man."

According to the paper's – admittedly biased – account of what happened next, Castanon and his party rented rooms at the Russell House hotel, located near where Ripley's Believe It Or Not stands today and sent for Reyes, who was working a short distance away, at the *El Republicano* office.

Reyes arrived at the hotel alone and unarmed for a "gentlemanly visit" with Castanon, only to be repeatedly insulted and possibly pushed

At the time of the crime...

During the incumbency of Monroe County Judge James Magbee, His Honor was arrested in Tampa for drunkenness and while incarcerated discovered a novel solution to this dilemma. Magbee issued a writ of habeas corpus that commanded Tampa mayor J.E. Lipscomb to "bring the body of James Magbee before His Honor James Magbee, to show by what authority he was depriving him of his liberty." The mayor ignored the writ and upon his release Magbee threatened to jail the mayor for contempt of court. It never happened.

around a little. He left immediately.

Upon hearing of the incident, hundreds of local Cubans assembled in the street outside the hotel and began shouting profanities at the window of Castanon's room. So furious was this mob that the police were called in to disperse it.

"Castanon has come as a conquistador to this peaceful city, and has stained the flag of stars and stripes, following his intentions to create confusion through his dirty newspaper," proclaimed *El Republicano*.

• • •

The next day brought new developments.

According to a later edition of *El Republicano* Reyes decided to accept Castanon's challenge of a duel to the death, but was arrested before the deed could take place. Other Key West Cubans stepped forward to fill the void and Castanon eventually agreed to a duel with a man named Orozco provided that it occurred "within the city limits, inside a house, with revolver and knife, chest to chest, to death."

Around noon, the designated witnesses went to the Russell House with a copy of the "rules" that had been agreed to for Castanon to sign, only to find that he had changed his mind. The duel was off and Castanon was now merely biding his time, waiting with his comrades for the arrival of the steamer New Orleans so that they could return to Cuba.

Once again an angry crowd filled the street outside the hotel, taunting Castanon and urging him to follow through with his earlier promise to fight one of their own. But Castanon was adamant: There would be no duel after all.

Around 11 a.m. the next day Orozco went to the Russell House to demand an explanation from Castanon. The two men met in the hotel lounge, facing the street and proceeded to argue. According to *El Republicano*, again, not the most unbiased source, Castanon slapped his adversary in the face. Orozco reciprocated and before long Castanon had pulled out a gun and opened fire. Orozco, who was unarmed, jumped outside where someone in the crowd handed him a pistol. Castanon by now had climbed the stairs to the second floor, his gun blazing. Orozco, however, was the better shot and he managed to hit Castanon in the lip and groin.

"Viva Espana con honra!" (or "long live Spain with honor") Castanon was said to have shouted, imitating a Spanish warrior, before falling down dead.

Naturally, the Cuban papers loyal to Spain considered Castanon's killing an "assassination" and they related a very different version of his death. In their account, a defenseless Castanon was all but ambushed outside the hotel by angry locals and murdered. Regardless of which story is true, one thing is certain: Upon his death, Castanon became an instant martyr to the cause of Spanish rule in Cuba and his offspring "the children of the mother country."

According to the pro-Spanish Cuban newspaper *Diarios de la Marino*, "The steamer Lavala that brought the body [arrived] in port with the flag flying at half-mast and as it passed national war ships came the tunes of a funeral march . . . ."

■ ■ ■

But the story of Don Gonzalo Castanon doesn't end there.

In an interesting postscript, his influence on Cuban politics was undoubtedly greater from beyond the grave – though not in the way he would have wanted.

Not long after he was buried in Havana in a large mausoleum befitting a Spanish loyalist hero, 41 medical students from the University of Havana were arrested for – allegedly – vandalizing his grave.

Thirty-three of the students were sentenced to imprisonment and/or hard labor, but eight of their classmates were executed by firing

The Castanon/Reyes Affair

squad on Nov. 27, 1871. So brutal was this atrocity in the eyes of the Cuban people that the incident became a rallying point for Cuban independence heroes such as Jose Marti – especially when it turned out that the charges against the students had been a sham in the first place.

When the island finally gained its formal liberty from Spain in 1902, it was in some small measure due to Castanon – and that cradle of Cuban liberty, Key West. ◁

A MONUMENT TO MARTYRS:
A memorial to eight students executed for profaning Don Gonzalo de Castanon's grave is located in the Colon Cemetery next to Revolution Square in the Vedado neighborhood of Havana. Another memorial to the students can be found on the Malecon, Havana's waterfront boulevard.

True Crime Stories of Key West and the Florida Keys, Vol. 2

Photo courtesy of Mary and Erin Bäcker
Capt. Rolf Bäcker in port with the *Ocean Clipper* in 1989.

America's Most Wanted

The Monroe County Sheriff's Office had no luck tracking down this elusive murder suspect. That is, until John Walsh got ahold of the case . . . .

America's Most Wanted

Since its debut in 1988, "America's Most Wanted" has helped put away hundreds of murderous criminals and made this country a much safer place. It's rare, however, that a case from the Florida Keys makes it on this popular TV show. We just don't get as much violent crime as we did in the 1970s and '80s when the economy was in the tank and many drug smugglers and dealers seemed almost immune to prosecution.

Nowadays, the Keys see one, maybe two murders per year and the killers are almost always caught immediately. Once in a while, though, somebody comes along who necessitates the kind of citizen's APB that "America's Most Wanted" provides.

This is the story of one such case.

• • •

On the morning of April 5, 1991, Key West shrimp boat captain Rolf Bäcker loaded his 70-foot vessel *Ocean Clipper* with enough fuel and ice for a two-week trip, recruited a mate from the Stock Island docks, kissed his wife Mary goodbye and set off for the Gulf Coast shrimping grounds. He had originally set out on the trip on April 1, but as fate would have it, had been forced by mechanical failure to return to port for repairs.

Bäcker was an experienced captain who had arrived in Key West in 1973 and worked aboard various shrimp boats until he had saved enough money to buy the *Clipper* in '76.

Three years later, the industrious German immigrant and his wife had put enough cash away to buy a house.

Bäcker was described as a stable and devoted father to his three children and an attentive husband to Mary, whom he had met at the Eden Roc Hotel in Miami Beach, while on his way to Key West. He was also kind. During the 1980 Mariel Boatlift, he went to Cuba and brought back 365 refugees on his boat and was seen crying when the Cuban authorities harshly dumped an elderly and ailing woman on his deck.

In short, Bäcker, who had arrived in town with $20 in his pocket, was a self-made Key West success story.

And so, when his regular mate couldn't make the trip that fateful day in April, he had no qualms about giving another man – who hadn't been in town long – an opportunity to fish.

■ ■ ■

Bäcker hadn't been expected back in Key West until April 18. And so, when Mary heard a rumor that her husband had suffered an injury a week or so after he had left she became worried. She called the Coast Guard and area hospitals, but nobody had heard a thing about Rolf being hurt.

Then, on April 13, Mary's world was turned upside down. The *Ocean Clipper* had been found abandoned near Cottrell Key, some three miles from Key West. Officers boarding the beached vessel discovered lots of blood and signs of a struggle in the cabin. Bäcker's last catch of shrimp, over 930 pounds, according to his hand-written log, was missing – as were Bäcker and his mystery mate. The log itself ended abruptly on April 10, several days before the stranded shrimp boat had been spotted.

"No body. Nothing," Monroe County Sheriff's Deputy Eddie Diaz told *Miami Herald* columnist Carl Hiaasen. "We're working it as a homicide."

Adding insult to injury, Mary Bäcker also found herself facing financial hardship. Steep fines had been levied by the federal government for every day the *Ocean Clipper* lay stranded in the tidal flats.

At the time of the crime...

On Oct. 29, 1991, Monroe County Judge Wayne Miller sentenced Key Wester Zachary Brown to listen to two hours of string orchestra music for blaring reggae on a downtown street corner. Brown was told to report to the library to "serve" his sentence and report back with a note from the librarian to prove he had done it.

Some of Bäcker's tools were salvaged and friends of the family George and Dorothy Sherman, among others, opened a relief fund for Mary and the kids at a local bank.

By the end of the month the grieving widow was looking at cleanup fines and fees in excess of a quarter of a million dollars. And Coast Guard officials were knocking on her door to collect.

"To me, it's like how much are they going to dump on this woman until she cracks," Bäcker family friend Lorraine Kilburn said. "It's not her fault. Why don't they try to find the jerk who did this?"

■ ■ ■

In fact, the sheriff's deputies working the case had been slowly piecing together what had happened. And all the evidence kept leading them back to the as-yet unidentified – and missing – mate. As news of Captain Bäcker's apparent murder spread throughout the fishing and boating community, the tips started rolling in. By the time Hiaasen's *Miami Herald* column ran on April 29, they were saying that the *Clipper* mate had hitched a ride to shore from a passing charter boat, telling the captain that Bäcker "had been removed from his boat 'by an unknown party and treated for a broken leg.'"

On May 7, the sheriff's office released a photo of 33-year-old Richard Flowers, aka Ricky Lee Flowers/Richard Thompson, whom they were looking for "in connection with" Bäcker's disappearance. But Flowers, who had been the mate on Bäcker's last shrimping tip, seemed to have disappeared and nobody could say where.

On May 15, the day after the *Key West Citizen* carried Rolf Bäcker's obituary, authorities at last had all the evidence they needed to issue a warrant for Flowers' arrest for first-degree murder. The "possible homicide" investigation was now a full-blown manhunt.

"I'm just glad that they're finally getting [a warrant] out," Mary Bäcker told the *Citizen*. "From the day that boat was found without my husband, I knew it was murder."

The warrant contained a number of revelations, such as the testimony of one witness that Flowers had traded a bag of shrimp for a 12-pack of beer upon his return to Key West. Other witnesses said that Flowers' story kept shifting. One minute he was telling them that Bäcker had "fallen down a ladder." Then he was saying that the "captain had been injured in a fight the two had in which they armed themselves with heavy tools."

Flowers was said to have returned to the doomed shrimp boat one day before it was found, and with the aid of two Stock Island men, pillaged nine large bags of shrimp. The men later sold the shrimp and Flowers bolted.

A short time after the warrant was issued, the case took an unexpected twist. "America's Most Wanted" announced that it would feature the case on an episode set to air May 31, 1991.

Anticipation and hope both ran high in Mary Bäcker.

"I'm really hoping this is going to get him," she said.

■ ■ ■

On the evening of Friday, May 31, Sheriff Lamar Echols of McIntosh County, Georgia, was flipping channels on his television when he saw something that stopped him cold. It was an AMW segment on a murder down in Key West, complete with photos of the suspect, Ricky Flowers.

The show over, Echols turned off his TV, got up and put on his guns. Duty called.

Less than an hour later, Flowers was in police custody awaiting an extradition hearing to send him back to the Southernmost City.

"I know Ricky," Echols told the *Citizen*. "He's got family here. He was real cooperative. . . which he's always been for us. We've arrested him over the years on little simple charges, but nothing like this."

He had a pretty good idea of where he might be, Echols said, and only had to knock on three doors before he found him.

Just before midnight, scant hours after the program aired, the producers of "America's Most Wanted" called Mary Bäcker to tell her that the man suspected of killing her husband was in custody and would soon stand trial. The speed of Flowers' arrest had come close to setting

America's Most Wanted

Bäcker aboard the *Clipper*.

Photo courtesy of Mary and Erin Bäcker

a record for the show.

"I just couldn't believe the fast results," Bäcker said. "It's just wonderful."

■ ■ ■

A little over a year later, on Aug. 11, 1992, Ricky Flowers finally admitted – in the Monroe County courtroom of Judge Richard Fowler – what everybody connected to the case already believed: He had killed Rolf Bäcker during a physical fight, then beached the *Ocean Clipper* and hitched a ride to shore with a passing vessel. Flowers made his confession as part of a plea deal that would see him sentenced to 12 years in prison and five years parole afterwards. His attorney, Bill Kuypers told the court that his client maintained that Bäcker's death had been an "accidental" occurrence during the course of the struggle. Flowers and

Bäcker had been feuding when the mate jumped overboard and tried to swim to another boat, to return to land. Having failed in his attempt, he returned to the *Clipper* where, he claimed, Bäcker hit him with a wrench. He responded in kind with a crowbar and the fight escalated from there. After he realized that he had killed the captain, Flowers said he panicked and threw the body overboard.

Mary Bäcker didn't believe a word of it. "My husband would be legally blind without his glasses, and they were left behind in his room," she said. "He was hit in the back of the head with one of those large, plumber's-type wrenches. I believe it was pre-meditated murder, though we can't prove it."

The prosecution, for their part, seemed to think they were getting the best deal they could, as Flowers pleaded guilty to second-degree murder.

"It was a good resolution considering we did not have a body, and [the evidence] was circumstantial," Prosecutor John Ellsworth said.

By this time, Mary Bäcker's situation has stabilized somewhat. The previous November she had finally been able to obtain a death certificate for her slain husband, making her eligible for Social Security and other benefits, as she struggled to raise her children alone. She had also made up her mind to remain in Key West rather than returning to her parents' home in Minnesota as she had previously planned. To assist her in this endeavor, the state had also required that Flowers pay $50,000 restitution to Bäcker's widow for the loss of income and hardship he had caused. He was also ordered to pay for all costs associated with the grounding of the *Ocean Clipper*. Ellsworth cautioned Mary Bäcker, however, that she'd likely never receive any money.

"I never did receive a cent because he never got a job," Mary Bäcker said.

All told, Mary Bäcker wasn't thrilled with the deal, but she, like the prosecution, accepted that pushing for an unwinnable first-degree murder charge could have resulted in Flowers walking free. As it was, the case had languished for a year as the accused killer went through five different lawers.

"I wish [the sentence] could be higher," Bäcker said. "But I feel

John [Ellsworth] did the best he could under the circumstances."

• • •

The next month, on Sept. 16, 1992, Flowers appeared in court for formal sentencing. Having agreed to his plea deal the previous month, the hearing was a mere formality. Nonetheless, Mary Bäcker and her 14-year-old daughter Erin were in court for the occasion.

"When I see other children with their families, I can almost picture him with us, and this brings tears to my eyes because I remember how much we were a family," Erin Bäcker told Judge Fowler.

Mary Bäcker repeated her assertion that she wasn't "100 percent happy with it," but then made a prescient prediction: Flowers would screw up during his parole and end up back in the clink.

Flowers apologized to the Bäckers for their pain, but asserted that he was sticking to his version of events. Then he was led away to begin serving his sentence.

• • •

As it turned out, Mary Bäcker's prediction proved correct. After serving six years of his sentence, Flowers was released early for good behavior. Before long he returned to Key West where he took up passing bad checks. Eventually, he ended up back in the Monroe County Jail

Convicted killer Ricky Flowers is out of jail now; nobody knows where.

One thing is certain: Should he murder again, authorities know one proven way to try to find him. ⚓

MARITIME MOVIE STAR:
Rolf Bäcker and the *Ocean Clipper* can be seen in the opening sequence of the 1983 film "Scarface."

Photo courtesy of Monroe County Library
Manuel 'El Isleno' Cabeza in his U.S. Army uniform.

Killed by the Klan

Beaten, tarred and feathered by the Ku Klux Klan
for living with a mulatto woman,
Manuel 'El Isleno' Cabeza sought
bloody revenge. Some say his wish
came true – from beyond the grave . . . .

Killed by the Klan

As a welcoming port to ships, cargoes and crews from around the world, Key West has always been seen as a fairly tolerant place for minority cultures, even during its turn-of-the-19th-century heyday. Slavery, though practiced, was not as widespread, nor as important to the local economy as it was in the Deep South. In 1860, before the outbreak of the Civil War, many in Key West had actually tried to help scores of slaves liberated from three captured ships. An African cemetery and memorial at Higgs Beach today marks the final resting place of many of these unfortunates, who succumbed to disease and starvation during their grueling journey across the Atlantic.

Monroe County was still Dixie, however, and the town was not without its representatives of the Ku Klux Klan. The organization, considered a terrorist group by the federal government, reached its peak of membership and political power in the 1920s. It was during this time that its one and only documented lynching in the Southernmost City took place.

Accounts of the story vary, but one thing's for sure: The gruesome killing and its eerie aftermath continue to be the stuff of Key West legend.

• • •

Native Key Wester Manuel Cabeza was not a man to be messed with. Big, strong and handsome, Cabeza was known as "El Isleno," Spanish for "The Islander," as his Spanish family had moved to Key West from the Canary Islands off the west coast of North Africa.

Born in 1897, Cabeza served in the U.S. Army from November of 1917 to April 1919, receiving an honorable discharge. His conduct as a civilian however was not always considered honorable. In 1911 he had been severely cut by two others during a melee said to be sparked by a discussion of politics. The following year El Isleno was arrested for assaulting police officer Thomas Lowe – with intent to kill. Somehow he remained free. Eventually World War I intervened and Cabeza was shipped off to battle.

Upon his return to Key West from the conflict, Cabeza, then in his early twenties, became a larger than life figure in the small community. The muscular combat vet owned and operated the Red Rooster, "described variously as a bar, a coffee shop and a sporting club," according to a 1994 article in *Sunshine* magazine by Florida historian Stuart McIver. The establishment was located on Thomas Street, not far from a Key West seaport then awash in bordellos and contraband rum-soaked speakeasies. In his free time, Cabeza was said to be a player and lady-killer.

"He was one of those men what likes to spend their money for a good time, drinking and all that," his friend Norberto Diaz told writer Stetson Kennedy in 1939. "But he never caused nobody no trouble; all he did was to be happy and enjoy life."

Still, there was another side to Cabeza, one that had been hinted at by his earlier brushes with the law. Powerful and intimidating as a Category-5 hurricane, "El Isleno" was said to have something of an outlaw folk-hero streak.

He "got to be known as the Robin Hood," another Key West old-timer Perucho Sanchez recalled. "He took care of some of the poor black families back of Whitehead Street. He'd bust into the gambling rooms, grab the money on the table and give it to the poor – nobody fought him. He was a mean, tough hombre."

At the time of the crime...

On June 26, 1926 Puerto Rican-born Key Wester Lorencio "A Dice" Ortega committed a classic "Cuban crime of passion" when he shot and killed his ex-girlfriend Mercedes Carmancha and her new lover Manuel Jiminez at the intersection of Whitehead Street and Truman Avenue. Ortega was arrested a month later in New York City and eventually sentenced to 20 years in prison.

To top things off, Cabeza began living with his mulatto lover – a former prostitute named Angela. This was an absolute disgrace to certain elements of the white community, who nonetheless had no problem with "their kind" pleasuring themselves with non-white mistresses and whores.

El Isleno's behavior, taking place as it did during Prohibition, (a cause near and dear to the hearts of Klan members,) was certain to raise eyebrows. Eventually, it raised hell itself.

Photo courtesy of Monroe County Library
Alleged Key West Ku Klux Klan leader William Decker.

■ ■ ■

It began with a warning, according to Norberto Diaz, to get Angela out of his house.

"But Isleno wasn't afraid of nobody," Diaz said. "When he got that warning he just started keeping his gun under the counter of his shop."

Their warning unheeded, the Klan decided to send Cabeza a message he couldn't ignore.

On Dec. 23, 1921, as he lay in bed with his Angela, a half-dozen cars pulled up to their residence and burst into their apartment. They subdued Cabeza with clubs and their fists, then threw him into one of the waiting cars and headed for the outskirts of town. There they continued the beating, before tarring and feathering the young man and ordering him to leave town – on pain of death.

Merry Christmas.

The Klan had got the better of El Isleno through sheer force of numbers, but during the course of the attack, the victim had managed to pull the masks off a few of the men.

That evening, as he lay in bed, "in agony from a burst kidney," according to Stuart McIver's account, "Angela reached back into her Afro-Cuban heritage to call up the gods of voodoo. In the candlelight, she made a sacrifice of chickens, blood and bones. She screamed her curse on the Klansmen of Key West: Violent death to all who had harmed her husband."

The next day, on the morning of Christmas Eve, Cabeza took matters into his own hands.

Still in horrible pain from his ordeal, he hired a taxi and drove to the railroad station in search of one of the men, who worked as a baggage handler there. The man was lucky: He had been given Christmas Eve off.

Next, Cabeza – gun in hand – ordered the cabbie to cruise around Old Town as he searched for the other Klansmen he had recognized. As they drove north on Duval Street, they passed a car driven by William Decker, manager of a local cigar factory – and allegedly the head of the Key West Klan. Cabeza ordered the taxi driver to turn the cab around and overtake Decker. As they pulled alongside the vehicle, Cabeza leaned out of the cab and opened fire, shouting, "Decker, this is how a man kills a man!"

"The Islander shot the Klansman through the jaw," according to Stuart McIver. "He slumped over the wheel of the car, dead on the spot." Decker's Ford jumped the curb and hit a phone pole outside the Cuban Club, scattering terrified pedestrians from the sidewalk like scared stray cats. The dressed turkey Decker had bought for his family's Christmas dinner sat where he had left it, on the back seat of his car.

Cabeza, having hit his mark, ordered his cabbie to drive on. The

Islander jumped out at Petronia and Whitehead streets and quickly climbed to a top floor cupola of a corner building owned by the Solano family, where a group of citizens, including many armed Klansmen and some Marines, was gathering.

"[Cabeza] began firing at the crowd," the *Miami Herald* reported on Dec. 26, 1921. "One bullet grazed Police Captain Roker's ear. Another just missed Eddie Page. The cupola . . . has four windows, facing all directions, so he was able to fire at the crowd from four directions, creating a great commotion." At the same time, the Klansmen, incensed at the slaying of one of their own, were blasting the cupola with buckshot.

As Sheriff Roland Curry drove to the U.S. Naval Station to procure a Marine machine gun team, several lawmen were dispatched to try to persuade Cabeza to surrender peacefully.

The Islander was no fool, however and refused to deal with anyone other than Chief Deputy McInnis, whom he knew personally and trusted to take care of him.

"'I'll come down McInnis,'" the *Herald* quoted Cabeza saying, "'Because I know that you will protect me.' And with that remark, he jumped down and grabbed McInnis by the arm, seeking his protection."

Cabeza was taken to the Monroe County Jail a few blocks away at the corner of Whitehead and Fleming streets and placed in a cell. Armed Marines stood guard around the jail – more to keep the crowd out than to keep Cabeza, who now feared for his life, in. Around 1 a.m, however, Sheriff Curry, "thought by some to be a racist," according to McIver, told the Marines he had the situation in hand and that they could go home to their families.

What followed was one of the most disturbing events in the history of the Florida Keys.

■ ■ ■

In the early morning hours of Christmas Day, 15 or so men entered the unguarded jail and headed straight for El Isleno's unlocked cell. They beat him senseless with blackjacks and baseball bats as other inmates cowered in their cells, then dragged him out and tied him to a car bumper. The Klansmen dragged Cabeza, who was probably already dead, all the way out to a deserted area called "the Dam," near what is today the Key West International Airport. There they lynched him and – just to be sure – peppered the once proud and strong Islander with buckshot and bullets.

"A bloody, bludgeoned body hanging from a tree was the Klan's Christmas Day gift to Key West," McIver wrote.

• • •

A grand jury was convened to look into the matter, but no one was ever charged with Cabeza's murder. Adding insult to injury, the court claimed that given El Isleno's demeanor and his "affront to society" of living with a mulatto woman, he pretty much deserved what he got.

"He had a very bad reputation," the grand jury wrote. "His name was a terror to officers of the law . . . and to the citizens in general."

In addition, the jury concluded that Cabeza had killed the wrong man, as William Decker had been seen at the Elks Club at the time of El Isleno's tarring and feathering.

El Isleno was dead. His lover's curse, however, lived on.

In 1939, Cabeza's friend Norberto Diaz told the writer Stetson Kennedy that "Angela's curse has already killed five of the Ku Klux Klan who beat and hung Isleno. Cabeza shot the Klan leader himself, one man was blown up by dynamite when he was working on the bridges, another got caught in the Matecumbe hurricane, one was ground to pieces under his boat when it went on a reef and another went fishing and never came back. The curse killed them all. It's killing another with tuberculosis now."

Killed by the Klan

The fate of Sheriff Curry in particular epitomized the supposed outcome of the curse. He was the man Diaz mentioned as having been "ground to pieces under his boat." According to Monroe County historian Tom Hambright the lawman was left in such excruciating pain from the accident that he needed to be cut from the wreckage and spent the final few days of his life in unparalleled and unrelenting agony.

The curse may or may not have killed the men. One thing is certain: None of them lived to lynch again . . . . ▲

A FATHER'S CURSE:

In June of 1968 *Key West Citizen* columnist F.E.B. claimed to have been given the transcript of an additional curse placed upon the entire island of Key West by El Isleno's father: It read,

"Oh God, let this beautiful island falsely prosper with good things, fair weather smugness and freedom to play and to love. But then, Almighty God, always rip from this island the sweetness . . . As the cruel equator's sun burns the pink skin of the northern visitor, please, blight each business undertaking, slay the men who go off to wars, make friendships to perish, and houses to blaze containing the prissy possessions of those who are not wise enough to know that one cannot posses . . . Make happy island laughs turn into groans . . . Let every pillow be wet with the loss of a loved one. May a vicious disease strike and destroy while the cool island zephyrs sigh over the lonely and damned island people."

Another *Citizen* columnist, Earl Adams, claimed this curse was a fake. He did concede that Cabeza's father, kneeling at his son's grave, prayed that "those responsible for my son's death may die a thousand times more painful death."

It seems that he – and Angela – got their wish.

True Crime Stories of Key West and the Florida Keys, Vol. 2

Photo courtesy of Monroe County Library
Harry Powell, right, is sworn in as a Key West city commissioner by Mayor Richard Heyman and fellow Commissioner Virginia Panico in 1987.

A Short Fuse

Renegade City Commissioner Harry Powell set out to 'keep Peary Court green.' His methods had half the town – and the U.S. government – seeing red . . . .

A Short Fuse

Key Westers have had a symbiotic yet complicated relationship with the U.S. Navy for nearly two centuries. The cheers that heralded the arrival of Commodore David Porter's West Indies Anti-Pirate Squadron in 1823 turned quickly to jeers, as Porter assumed dictatorial powers and allowed his men to abscond with residents' private property.

Over the years, the townsfolk have benefited from Navy dollars yet fought with sailors over girls; they've pressed the Navy fire department into service when needed then turned around and cursed their annexation of scarce island land.

This "can't live with 'em, can't live without 'em" mindset has produced a few memorable rows over the years. During a period in the early '90s, one such dispute divided the town – and very nearly became an explosive situation . . .

■ ■ ■

Peary Court straddles the unofficial dividing line between Old Town and New Town in the area bordered by White Street to the west, Palm Avenue to the north and Garrison Bight to the east. The 29-acre tract has been owned by the government since the 1820s. During the mid-1970s, dilapidated military housing on the site was torn down, creating one of the few open park spaces in an increasingly urban Key West. The Navy gave the city a sweetheart lease on the land in 1974, which over the years opened the door for such improvements as tree planting and a concession stand for the ball field.

In time Peary Court, named for the Arctic explorer Robert Peary, came to be regarded by dog-walkers and softball players as THEIR space, the "Central Park of Key West," as one woman put it.

But a time bomb was ticking . . . .

With the booming city increasingly becoming a resort town of high off-base rents – and the ramping up of Caribbean anti-drug interdiction efforts during the Reagan years, the Navy and Coast Guard claimed to once again need Peary Court for military housing. They served notice to the city commission in the mid-1980s that 160 units of housing were planned and prepared for a seamless takeover of the park which, incidentally, contained a Civil War-era cemetery.

As bids for the construction were sent out and the time for the handover grew near, Key Westers became increasingly belligerent. Why did the Navy need to build here, anyway? Wasn't there plenty of buildable space on Navy-occupied land at Trumbo Point and Sigsbee? Or for that matter, at Boca Chica, a few miles up the Keys?

Among the activists loudly denouncing the Navy's actions was City Commissioner Harry Powell, first elected to his position in 1987. As public demonstrations against the Navy's move broke out in early 1990, Powell's was a prominent face among the dissenters.

"We want the Navy and bidders to be forewarned," he said ominously in a March 13 *Key West Citizen* interview, "that we are not giving up ship."

■ ■ ■

By late November of 1990 the Navy made it official. Naval Air Station Key West Commander Capt. Jack Ensch sent City Manager Felix Cooper a letter advising him that as of Dec. 1, civilians would no longer be permitted to enter the grounds excepting persons doing business with the credit union, located on a cul de sac in the heart of Peary Court. Get rid of park improvements such as the bleachers and softball field or we'll do it for you, was the gist of the letter.

At the time of the crime...

On Dec. 20, 1994, Key West police arrested Eric Bissell, 33, for "allegedly firing a cannon from his Whitehead Street balcony in the direction of a group of workers," the *Key West Citizen* reported. Bissell had had a run-in with the workers earlier in the day. He told the cops that he had received the cannon, which made a booming noise, but didn't launch a projectile, for his birthday the week before. Bissell was charged with discharging a firearm in public and making, possessing and discharging a destructive device.

Again, Harry Powell made his feelings known, agreeing that the city should remove the fencing, lighting, press box and concession stand, not to concede the skirmish to the Navy, but rather, to dig in for a long fight.

"It's a battle," he ominously told the *Citizen* on Nov. 27. "And in a battle you don't leave your fine china upstairs, you put it in the basement."

By now, Powell's increasingly militant language was beginning to find its counterpoint among many pro-Navy locals. As if in response to the commissioner's near declaration of war, the press box at Peary Court was gutted by a Dec. 2 fire that Key West Assistant Fire Chief Dennis Wardlow called "suspicious," and caused by "some type of flammable liquid." No investigation was planned.

Powell wasn't shook.

"Let's hope this thing rises from the ashes," he said. "That battle will go on, regardless."

■ ■ ■

Shortly before midnight on Sunday, Nov. 2, a 21-year-old protester named Molly Ellen Logan scaled a rubber tree at Peary Court, threaded a bike lock through her jeans and chained herself to a branch. Brandishing several placards and screaming "Keep Peary Court Green," Logan greeted the armed military police the next morning as they arrived for their first day on the job, "securing" the park for the upcoming construction project. The Navy's headache had entered a new phase. Tour buses were stopping; a Conch Train driver was diverting from the usual route to swing his passengers by Key West's newest – and hottest – tourist attraction. And the protesters were growing into a small tent city. Among its inhabitants was Commissioner Harry Powell.

"The city and citizens of this community have not been treated fairly," Powell told the *Miami Herald* on Dec. 5. "I can understand Molly Logan's frustration . . . I personally applaud her." Not to be outdone, Powell's colleague, Commissioner Jimmy Weekley, and state Senator

Larry Plummer climbed up into Logan's perch to show their solidarity. Key West Mayor Captain Tony Tarracino also expressed his support, saying he had a "tremendous amount of respect for Logan. If we didn't have people like that this country wouldn't be what it is today."

By Dec. 7, the Navy had had enough. Armed men pulled Logan down from the tree and hauled her into the federal courthouse on Simonton Street where she was charged with trespassing on federal land. Logan was released on a $50,000 surety bond after requesting a jury trial. Ultimately, she was acquitted when U.S. Magistrate the Hon. Lurana S. Snow agreed with defense attorney Nathan Eden's assertion that Logan hadn't been trespassing at the time she climbed into the tree.

■ ■ ■

For a couple of years things quieted down some as construction on the housing was delayed by a lawsuit filed by Key West environmental group Last Stand.

But by the fall of 1992 with the project slated to get underway, Powell, by now a private citizen, took matters into his own hands.

At one point, Powell pedaled his conch cruiser bike onto the disputed land, chained himself to the bike and held a press conference for about 20 protesters standing at the site. As he finished speaking, two Navy vehicles pulled up and asked him to leave. He refused, informing them that he was chained to his bike.

Key West Police Chief Ray Peterson cut the chain and placed Powell in the back of a paddy wagon. After posting $180 bail, he was set free. But Powell's career as an outlaw dissident had officially begun.

■ ■ ■

At the dawn of 1994, construction on the Navy's housing was in progress. With all legal appeals exhausted, the mood of the project's opponents was one of weary resignation. How many battles does the average citizen ever win against the U.S. government, anyway?

Average citizens, it seemed, hadn't counted on Harry Powell.

Around 7 o'clock on the morning of Jan. 13, Powell packed up a stick of dynamite, three blasting caps and a two-gallon can of gasoline and rode his bicycle from his house on Whitehead Street across town to Peary Court, stopping to drop a letter in a friend's mailbox along the way. The letter stated that he had strapped dynamite to his chest and was in possession of detonators including a "dead man's switch."

Once at the site, Powell broke into a trailer belonging to the construction company and called his friend to tell him to look in his mailbox. His next call was to the Key West Police Department, threatening to blow himself and the trailer up and demanding a federal inquiry into the Navy's plans for Peary Court. Specifically, why did they need to build it there and then, during an era of military cutbacks?

For nine and a half hours the ex-commissioner barricaded himself in the trailer giving interviews to various media outlets and negotiating his surrender with a SWAT team.

He had no plans to actually use the explosives, he insisted, telling the *Miami Herald* "I'm not a violent person," as a crowd of 50 or so supporters continued to gather around Peary Court.

"I did everything I could," Powell told the paper. "I spent five years writing letters, doing the research. I've fulfilled my part of the bargain. Our elected officials have not. This project is wrong for Key West. It's illegal, it's an environmental nightmare and it's wasteful."

Outside, the protesters carried signs that read "Give 'em hell, Harry," "We love you, Harry," and "Make Peary Court Green Again."

A backlash was growing, however. Around 20 patrons of Charlie's Place bar on Kennedy Drive wore hastily printed T-shirts, which read, "Stop the fight, give Harry a light."

"The whole bar had them on," bartender Christina Boeder told the *Citizen*. "We were chanting 'two, four, six, eight . . . come on, Harry, detonate.'"

The scene was repeated downtown at Durty Harry's Bar on Duval Street, which held a "Get Bombed" all-you-can-drink party, at a cost of $7.

Around 5:40 p.m., after securing a promise from the General Accounting Office and U.S. Senator Connie Mack to look into the need for the housing, Powell finally surrendered peacefully to the cops. The situation defused, he was immediately arrested and charged with possession of a destructive device, threatening to discharge a projectile and armed burglary — charges carrying a potential sentence of life in prison. Across the country, media reports were abuzz with the sensational story of this enigmatic former public servant's one-man crusade against the iron will of the mightiest military in the world.

■ ■ ■

At Powell's arraignment the next day, Monroe County Judge Wayne Miller ordered the activist held without bail pending his trial.

"When you have a person who goes to the extent of creating a bomb, there's no assurance his frustrations will not continue," State Attorney Kirk Zuelch explained.

As Powell languished in jail, his supporters threw a series of benefit parties in his name. Thousands were being raised for his legal defense, which was to be undertaken by crack Key West lawyer Michael Halpern.

On Feb. 3, Powell pleaded "not guilty" to the charges and began to hint at an insanity defense. Despite his assurances that he was by now stable and not a danger to the community, his request for bail was again denied.

For his part, Halpern revealed that Powell had deliberately neglected to bring to the trailer nitromethane which would have been required to set off the dynamite, rendering it harmless.

"It's fertilizer, something you can put in the ground and grow grass," he said. "Harry Powell had the great ability to grow plants in that trailer."

Judge Richard Fowler wasn't buying it.

"There is some concern on the part of the court that Mr. Powell may have gotten better at it in the meantime," he said.

A Short Fuse

∎ ∎ ∎

By late February, attorney Halpern made it official that he intended to use the insanity defense, a long shot at best, in states such as Florida. Powell's trial was to be delayed until sometime in May, until which time he would remain incarcerated in the Monroe County Jail.

Following several judge recusals and some backroom dealing with the State Attorney's Office, Powell on May 16 finally stood before Monroe County Judge William Ptomey and agreed to a deal that would see him spend no more than four years in jail in exchange for a guilty plea to charges of possessing a destructive device, threatening to discharge a destructive device, and transporting explosives. He also agreed to pay $16,001 in restitution and remain on probation for 13 years.

"I think it was just time to stand up and say 'yeah, I did it,'" Powell said at the time. "I just want to get on with my life. I'll still be a Key Wester. I just want to go back to work and live a happy life."

In July of 1994 Powell was formally sentenced to two years in prison, the minimum sentence under guidelines from the state. After serving time first at the South Florida Correctional Institute in South Miami and then the Madison Correctional Institution in North Florida, he was released on Oct. 25, in time to watch the wacky 16th annual Fantasy Fest parade file past his Whitehead Street home.

He had lost his battle to save his beloved park and except for an incident six months later, when he was picked up at an offshore buoy by a passing boat – after the sinking of his own – Powell has managed to keep a low profile in town.

Peary Court, too, has faded in importance in the public consciousness as new development battles have arisen and the post 9/11 climate has effectively blunted much criticism of policy decisions by the Navy and the armed forces in general.

For many Key Westers, though, the events of January 1994 are a reminder of a time when the conch still roared, a redux of the 1982 declaration of independence that birthed the Conch Republic and revealed the stubborn independent streak of its unconventional inhabitants.

As former Last Stand president Jim Farrell put it on the day of Powell's plea bargain, "The interest will drop in the community, but memories will linger. They'll always be there. It will take a long time for people to forget."

'DIRTY' HARRY POWELL BECOMES 'THE ENFORCER:'

Shortly after his retirement from the Key West City Commission in November of 1991, Harry Powell made a name for himself as a neighborhood vigilante. In early December of that year he shot and killed an errant rooster who was keeping his neighborhood awake at night. A week later he and a friend made a citizens' arrest of a local crack dealer. In response, a local radio DJ began calling Powell "The Enforcer," the title of the third installment in Clint Eastwood's "Dirty Harry" film series.

A Short Fuse

True Crime Stories of Key West and the Florida Keys, Vol. 2

Photo from the author's collection

Count Karl Tanzler Von Cosel, in black, with hat.

One Count of Weirdness

Karl Von Cosel was arrested for the strangest, most shocking crime in Key West history. Stranger still, many residents were sympathetic to his plight . . . .

One County of Weirdness

The story of Count Karl Von Cosel and his obsession with a deceased Key West beauty is probably the most famous, most written-about saga in the annals of Florida Keys history. It has been celebrated in songs like, "Ballad of Elena/She Was Pickled," by Ben Harrison; in books such as Harrison's *Undying Love*, *Ghosts of Key West*, by David Sloan and *A Halloween Love Story*, by Rod Bethel; as well as in numerous newspaper and magazine articles over the years – especially around Halloween. While most observers have focused on the bizarre nature of Von Cosel's actions, the legal aspects of the case are equally intriguing; it's that dimension of the tale that makes it worthy of inclusion in this volume.

■ ■ ■

From a legal standpoint, the story began on Oct. 7, 1940. For it was on that afternoon that Von Cosel, then 70, was formally charged with "malicious and wanton disfigurement of a burial vault in the city cemetery, when he removed the body of Elaine Hoyo Mesa (sic) to his home in defiance of state health laws," according to the *Key West Citizen*.

Just a day earlier it had been revealed that Von Cosel, a 10-year resident of Key West, had removed the body of the young woman, whom he considered his "sweetheart" in life, from her tomb at the cemetery seven years previously and taken her back to his home. There, he set about preserving her remains with wax and plaster of Paris. This instance of what most folks would call "grave-robbing" was discovered by the Monroe County authorities two weeks earlier as they investigated reports of vandalism in the cemetery. One of these reports had been filed by relatives of Elena Hoyos Mesa, as she was properly known, as they had been suspicious for some time that her body was not in the vault where she had been interred.

Acting on a hunch, Deputy Sheriffs Bernard Waite and Ray Elwood drove out to the reclusive and eccentric Von Cosel's Flagler Avenue house where they made a shocking discovery: The body of Elena lay perfectly preserved beneath a veil of mosquito netting, looking not all that different from the day she died.

"Then followed the train of events, just now uncovered, which at once lifts von Cosel to a position of national interest and, except for the gruesome aspects of the case, to recognition as one of the truest romantics of all time," the *Citizen* reported of "the crime, as some called it."

The paper's sympathy was easily evident. If Von Cosel was being tried in the press, he couldn't have asked for a better judge and jury.

■ ■ ■

Count Karl Tanzler Von Cosel, a scientist by training, had arrived in Key West in 1930 seeking to fulfill a prophecy that had come to him in a series of dreams in his native Germany. In these dreams, the "poor nobleman" had encountered a bewitchingly beautiful woman. One day when he awoke, he vowed to search the world until he found her. Eventually, this quest brought him to the Southernmost City, where he got a job as an X-ray machine operator at the Marine Hospital on Eaton Street. It was there, in this most unlikely of places, where he finally came face to face with his dream girl . . . but under less than optimal conditions. Elena Hoyos Mesa, then just 19, was suffering from tuberculosis — and the prognosis was bleak.

Von Cosel had attended to the dying beauty to no avail. Two years after being admitted to the hospital, she breathed her last and was bur-

At the time of the crime...

On July 12, 1941 the *Key West Citizen* reported that Sheriff Berlin Sawyer was "keeping close surveillance on two alleged houses of prostitution in the county." One of them, Mom's Tea Room on Stock Island, was said to have been closed down entirely. "When I first went out there I told the proprietor that there must not be any crooked work in the place," Sawyer said.

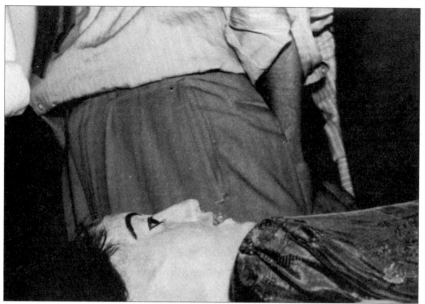

Photo from the author's collection
The remains of Elena Hoyos Mesa, as they were discovered at Von Cosel's home in October of 1940.

ied in a vault, built by Von Cosel with permission from Elena's father in the Key West City Cemetery. The "relationship" had never been consummated – in life.

• • •

For the dead girl's family there was nothing left to do but grieve, but Von Cosel had other ideas. Fretting that his beloved was in the process of decomposing into "nothingness," as the *Citizen* reported upon his arrest, the scientist eventually succumbed to his aching desire to be reunited with Elena. The better part of a decade after her untimely death, he busted into her mausoleum and carted her body off, by taxi, to his home in an area of town called the "Butcher Pens," near present-day Atlantic Boulevard and White Street. When that property sold, Von Cosel – and his beloved – moved out to the remote Flagler Avenue house.

It was there that the cops found her on that October morning in 1940.

• • •

Due perhaps to the bizarre nature of the case, county officials took their time exploring their legal options before formally arresting Von Cosel the day after the discovery. Bond was set at $1,000. Even as Von Cosel sat in a holding cell on Oct. 7 and 8 awaiting his hearing, hundreds of morbidly obsessed Key Westers and visitors were filing past Elena's remains at the Lopez Funeral Home – where the deceased's relatives were hastily planning a secret second burial. According to the *Citizen* it was understood that regardless of the outcome of the legal proceedings, Von Cosel would never be allowed to keep custody of Elena's remains.

Still, the paper reported that "Sympathy on all sides were expressed today for the aged scientist, and the general hope advanced was that the state would see fit to free him of the charges which keep him in the country prison."

For his part, Von Cosel was said to be "reconciled to cooperation with state officials."

If convicted of the pending charges, the aging scientist faced two years in jail and/or a fine of $500.

Fortunately for Von Cosel, he was going to get the best legal representation money could buy and it wasn't going to cost him a cent. Attorney Louis A. Harris, considered the "most experienced" lawyer in Key West by the *Citizen*, offered to represent the penniless perp at his Oct. 8 hearing, which lasted for nearly three hours in the courtroom of Peace Justice Enrique Esquinaldo.

Again, hundreds of Key Westers jammed the room to hear Von Cosel relate in a "low, steady voice" how he had tended to Elena during her illness and "promised her the day before she died that he would take care of her no matter what happened," according to the *Citizen*.

Under questioning by Harris, Von Cosel explained how he had

spirited the decomposing corpse to his residence and set about preserving what was left of Elena. He then stated that he would miss her terribly if she should be taken from him now.

Appearing as the chief witness against Von Cosel was Elena's sister, a Mrs. Mario Medina, who told the court how she had become suspicious 10 days previously that her sister was not in the crypt and had "accosted" the Count at his home, where she discovered the body. She had given the scientist one week to return Elena's remains. At the end of this grace period, she said, Von Cosel still steadfastly refused to give in. Only then had she called the authorities. Medina's testimony was corroborated by her husband and a friend named Oelinda Medina.

Following the hearing, the *Citizen* reported, "many observers were of the opinion that no trial would be held, rather that the defendant would be ordered confined in a sanatorium. This, [Judge] Esquinaldo refused to comment on."

He did, however, order Von Cosel held on his original bond while he considered his decision.

■ ■ ■

Three days later, Esquinaldo had made up his mind. Von Cosel would be held in custody for the next session of Criminal Court, scheduled for the next month, where he would face the charge of "wanton violation of a cemetery vault."

Again, Von Cosel got lucky when two sympathetic Key Westers, upon hearing of the decision, posted property as collateral sufficient to cover the $1,000 bond. Benjamin Fernandez and Joseph Zorsky sprang the scientist on Oct. 12 and issued a statement to the *Citizen*: "Persons in Key West who recall the circumstances surrounding Dr. Von Cosel's (sic) kindly administrations while Elena Hoyos Mesa was in the hospital have implicit faith in his motives.

"In appreciation of the service he rendered then, for his devotion to the girl he loved, and in behalf of the humanitarian aspects of this present case, I have followed my best judgement in assisting in furnishing bond for the defendant. We who know him think he should be freed of all charges."

• • •

By now, the strange case of the septegenarian grave-robber and his deceased dream girl was beginning to attract national attention – most of it sympathetic to Von Cosel.

On the afternoon of Oct. 15, the accused and his lawyer Harris dropped by the *Citizen* to show the publisher some of the supportive correspondence they claimed Von Cosel had been receiving.

From a Clara Mason in Hollywood, California, came this message:

"... The Sleeping Beauty ... lay in a glass case breathing ever so gently at Madame Tussard's (sic,) London, England. Twice I have visited her and hope to do so again as soon as the war is over. What on earth could be wrong in placing Dr. Von Cosel's 'Sleeping Beauty' in an airtight, glass case. She belongs to him absolutely. Is it not wonderful in this world of today to find such kindly thought? I have enclosed one dollar towards purchase of such a glass case."

Another letter came from a Mrs. Margo Nisbet of Flint, Michigan.

Her "vote would be in favor of letting Dr. Von Cosel keep her (Elena Hoyos Mesa's remains.) His great love for her must have been divine."

• • •

On the morning of Nov. 11, the sympathizers carried the day.

County prosecutor Allan B. Cleare, Jr. filed a "no-information bill," in the case, meaning that the county was declining to prosecute. Von Cosel was released and Elena's body was turned over to her family for burial.

This last action clearly annoyed Von Cosel, who apparently still had no idea what all the fuss was about. He loved her and he wanted her back. Period.

One County of Weirdness

In fact, when Von Cosel finally left Key West for good, he slammed the door behind him loudly: On the very afternoon he departed the city, the crypt where Elena had formerly been laid to rest exploded mysteriously. A couple of years later, Von Cosel's Flagler Avenue residence burned to the ground, also under inexplicable circumstances.

Von Cosel had beaten the rap. But he still didn't have Elena and he never would see her remains again.

It was with a broken heart – and a replica doll created to look like Elena – that Von Cosel died in July of 1952 in Zephyr Hills, Florida.

The story of the eternal love of the well-meaning but odd German scientist for his dead Key West beauty lives on. ♀

TELLING HIS TALE:

The first person to capitalize on the amazing story of Elena was Karl Von Cosel himself. Penniless and unemployable in his twilight years, he sold a piece entitled "The Secret of Elena's Tomb" to the pulp magazine "Fantastic Adventures." It was published in the Sept. 1947 issue and contained several factual inaccuracies.

True Crime Stories of Key West and the Florida Keys, Vol. 2

Photo courtesy of Monroe County Library

Deputy Key West Police Chief Raymond Casamayor on his way into the federal courthouse on Simonton Street, during the 'Bubba Bust' trial, in the summer of 1985.

The 'Bubba Bust'

The success of the 'Operation Conch' bust of Key West officials in the 1970s emboldened federal prosecutors to set up a second round of arrests. The high-profile follow-up trial made national news and changed Key West forever . . . .

'The Bubba Bust'

November 29, 1983 began as a typical business day at the Angela Street building that housed both the "new" Key West City Hall and the Key West Police Department.

Quickly the day became a historic milestone in the fight against organized crime and drug trafficking in the Keys.

As city employees and bystanders gaped, federal Grand Jury subpoenas were served to Deputy Police Chief Raymond Casamayor – the highest-ranking black official in town, with 28 years on the force – as well as detectives Russell Barker, Carroll Key and several others. The court documents demanded "all records relating to overtime, all payroll checks, time sheets, leave records, per diem expenses and travel reimbursements and any other payments . . . paid by the City of Key West, Florida for the period 1979 to present," according to the *Key West Citizen* of Dec. 2, 1983.

Something was up. And at least three of the men subpoenaed knew exactly what it was:

The "Bubba Bust," a RICO Statute case that sought to unravel a major cocaine distribution ring based in Key West – and punish those who had protected it – had rolled into town.

■ ■ ■

Key Westers had seen this sort of thing before. During Prohibition, the townspeople and local law enforcement turned a collective blind eye to the rum smuggling that kept the town afloat during the depths of the Great Depression. In the mid-1970s, the closing of the U.S. Navy's submarine base and its accompanying layoffs was the catalyst for a pot and cocaine smuggling bonanza that went largely unmolested by the State Attorney's Office. "Operation Conch," overseen by "outside" authorities, namely the U.S. Drug Enforcement Agency and the Florida Department of Law Enforcement had netted some notable convictions, such as that of Key West Fire Chief Joseph "Bum" Farto. For the most part, however, Key West remained a haven for drug smugglers and traffickers and their enablers in local police and government. Local juries remained reluctant to convict friends and family of the charges against them.

Adapting to this protective environment, the feds decided to try a different tack. This time around, as the accused "bubbas" looked up at the faces of the jurors deciding their fates, they would see not familiar smiles and winks, but a jury made up largely of residents of the northern part of the court district; folks who were increasingly concerned about bloody, cocaine-fueled street crime in Miami and its environs.

■ ■ ■

In total, more than 20 prominent Key Westers were formally charged in two separate Grand Jury indictments formally handed down on June 29, 1984, but in truth, the feds had been building their case for years. They'd collected boxes of records from the KWPD, and cut deals with drug dealers-turned informants, all in the hope of taking down the top "bubbas."

After a four-week trial that began on Oct. 19, 1984, eight defendants named in one of the indictments were found "not guilty." (One other had pleaded out prior to the trial.) To the public, it was starting to look like business as usual. But the "big show," featuring the three now-suspended cops, Casamayor, Barker and Key, as well as other local notables, was yet to begin.

At the time of the crime...

On May 23, 1985 the *Key West Citizen* reported that Eduardo Aquino of Islamorada claimed to have been walking beneath the Whale Harbor Bridge when he was approached by five Latin males wearing combat fatigues and brandishing automatic weapons. They asked Aquino if he was a member of Omega 7, an anti-Castro terrorist group. When he said he was not, Aquino was tied up and taken to a larger boat, where he was thrown over the side and shot at. He somehow managed to get loose and ran to a fishing camp to get help. Sheriff's investigators looked into the situation but by the next day found Aquino to be less cooperative. No arrests were ever made.

'The Bubba Bust'

By the time of the second trial, three defendants had pleaded out, leaving 14 defendants remaining.

Among those standing trial for a variety of drug-related charges were Carol Hardin, a school bus driver accused of smuggling cocaine in her bus; Key West lawyer (and former County Attorney) Michael Cates; his wife, Realtor Janet Hill Cates, a one-time Key West mayoral candidate; John R. Roberts; Buford E. Clark; Michael Alan Clark; Aristides M. Brito; Miguel Brito-Williams; Antonio Diaz; Oneri Fleita and Leon Edwards.

Jury selection began in late February of 1985 over the vociferous objections of Casamayor's Miami-based attorney Patricia Williams, that the jury pool contained not a single Monroe County resident. Her motion to dismiss the charges against her client – based on this exclusion of these "distinctive" citizens – was denied.

The trial began in early March in the Key West courtroom of U.S. District Court Judge C. Clyde Atkins. At the start, the prosecution, led by Assistant U.S. Attorneys Michael Sullivan and Eileen O'Connor suffered its own setback, as one of its star witnesses, Susan Avery, refused to be deposed. Avery was a close friend of Casamayor's who had fled to Australia from Key West after allegedly being intimidated by the suspended deputy chief. Scared for her life, she refused have any further involvement with the case.

Over the course of the next 10 weeks, Key Westers were treated to a sensational trial with elements of sex, drugs, Santeria magic, political intrigue, violence, racism and corruption.

The specifics of the charges and testimony were so lengthy and complicated that they could fill a separate book. At the onset of the trial, Casamayor alone was named in all 68 counts of the indictment. The essence of the trial, however, boiled down to this: The three cops were accused of taking bribes and protecting a $16 million Florida-wide coke distribution network involving the other defendants in one way or another. In addition, Casamayor faced charges of witness tampering and intimidation, tax evasion, and cocaine trafficking. During the course of the proceedings, some of these charges would be dropped, but there was

Photo courtesy of Monroe County Library
Casamayor carries his case to court with his attorney Patricia Williams.

no doubt that Casamayor's conviction was the biggest prize sought by the prosecution.

■ ■ ■

The first government witness, Carlos "Chuck" Nieves, told the court how he had ratted on his former partners in crime, Diaz and Brito-Williams, to Detectives Key and Barker following a White Street laundromat shooting in 1980. All were described as associates of the drug ring's kingpin, trafficker-turned government witness Hector Serrano, who was said to enjoy eating cocaine off a credit card several times per day.

Nothing appeared to have been done with the information, Nieves said.

Next up was one of the prosecution's big guns, Herb Reynolds, a former smuggler and Serrano partner, also turned government witness, who admitted injecting himself with coke up to 20 times per day.

Reynolds told the court that the indicted cops had all provided protection to himself and Serrano for years and that Serrano often delivered packages of cocaine to Casamayor – inside "Chicken Unlimited" boxes – at the Angela Street cop shop. In keeping with their protection arrangement, Reynolds said, the deputy chief had warned him to lie low when the F.B.I. came to town in 1981.

Reynolds also named six of the other defendants as customers of himself or Serrano. Michael Cates, the witness claimed, was on retainer as the legal advisor to the ring.

Next, the government brought forward a number of witnesses to testify to Casamayor's spending habits, attempting to justify the tax evasion charges by demonstrating that he spent way more than he earned. Witnesses admitted purchasing cashier's checks on his behalf, while merchants detailed renovation and remodeling work done at Casamayor's Key West home, as well as on two Big Pine Key properties he purchased in 1980.

Lewis Stark, a Daytona Beach state attorney, testified that following Reynolds' arrest for 140 grams of coke in April of '81, Casamayor called Stark no fewer than three times to recommend a sentence reduction based on Reynolds supposed work as an informant for the KWPD – thus shoring up the racketeering charges against the deputy chief.

Two days later prosecution witness Ofie Pazos, another former Serrano associate, detailed how he had delivered cocaine to four of the defendants, including Casamayor, setting the stage for testimony from Serrano himself.

Much of this incendiary testimony came in the form of tape recordings, made by Serrano, of his drug-related conversations with seven of the defendants – again including Casamayor – and Barker.

But it was under cross-examination that many of Serrano's darkest secrets came out. Questioned by Alvin Entin -- attorney for Leon Edwards, Oneri Fleita and Carol Hardin – Serrano admitted that he was involved in a 1976 terrorist bomb plot at Miami International Airport and that he had been approached by the CIA and DEA to assist them as a Cuban anti-communist fighter. He claimed that his Washington contact in this capacity was none other than CIA operative Frank Sturgis, the ex-Watergate burglar. Serrano began his large-scale cocaine trafficking in 1980, becoming an informant after being busted on drug charges in 1983. He had, however, been playing both sides of the fence prior to his arrest, working for the DEA while still selling coke.

"So you were helping the government on your right and dealing drugs with your left hand, is that not correct, Mr. Serrano?" Entin inquired, in an attempt to cast doubt on Serrano's credibility.

One after the other, defense attorneys jabbed away at Serrano but it seemed like the more he talked, the more he incriminated the defendants. Since he himself had immunity from prosecution he had nothing to lose by spilling his guts, admitting – among other things – that he had stuffed $1,000 in Detective Key's pocket, during a visit to the KWPD.

Next, government witness Wayne Kent detailed his days as a coke dealer with Miguel Brito and his relationship with both Cateses, saying that he and Janet came to be partners in the enterprise, buying up to a half-pound of the drug at a time for distribution. They also evolved into lovers, apparently with the stated approval of her husband.

He "pushed her on me," Kent testified. "He wanted me to date her, to take her out."

In June of 1980, Kent related, he had been shot in the stomach during a drug-related feud and was hospitalized for months. At this time, he said, Janet Cates brought him drugs in the hospital, and was "intimate" with him there, as well. All the while he was laid-up, she continued to run the drug business, he said. After the Cates couple eventually reconciled their marriage, Kent left the island in 1981.

A final prosecution witness, Key West Police Sergeant William McNeill reported that he had once asked Deputy Chief Casamayor for a piece of chicken from a Chicken Unlimited box on the latter's desk. Though the box appeared to be unopened, McNeill was informed that the chicken had already been eaten.

"I hope [Casamayor] gets 1,000 years," McNeill said, in concluding his testimony.

■ ■ ■

The prosecution's case, though damning, had one flaw, which the defense sought to exploit: It was mostly based on the word of drug dealers and other unsavory characters who had cut deals with the government to stay out of jail. In response, lawyers for the defense trotted out friends, family and business associates of the accused to try to dispel the impression that the accused were all drug-dealing gangsters. They also introduced testimony designed to infer a conspiracy on the part of the feds to "get" Casamayor.

In particular George Carey, a street-level cocaine dealer for Donald "The Candyman" Faison, testified that in 1975 he was busted by the Monroe County Sheriff's Office and "had been offered a deal if would sign a paper stating he was giving money to Casamayor to protect Faison's drug dealing," the *Citizen* reported. Earlier in the trial Faison had said that he had paid Casamayor protection money, but Carey had never delivered the cash personally and so refused to sign the statement.

Another figure from the past confirmed a similar experience. Convicted murderer and heroin dealer Bobby Francis, who had played a prominent role in Operation Conch a decade earlier, testified from his death row cell at Raiford State Penitentiary that upon his 1975 arrest, agents from the FDLE had offered to drop the drug charges if he would implicate Casamayor.

"When he told the authorities he hadn't had any dealings with Casamayor, the FDLE agents had stated they 'don't give a damn' whether or not Frances had any dealings with Casamayor,'" the *Citizen* wrote. Francis, like Carey, refused to sign. Both ended up facing drug charges.

Lifetime Key West resident Rose Kee, who with her husband John had lent Casamayor $5,000 towards the purchase of the Big Pine Key properties in 1980 called the deputy chief "a most outstanding police officer." The loan had been repaid, she added.

Another defense witness, Wayne Kent's neighbor John "Chuck" Weeks testified to Kent's temper and stated that he felt "Kent could not be trusted to tell the truth, even under oath," according to the *Citizen*.

This went on for weeks, with dozens of witnesses such as former Key West Mayor Dennis Wardlow and former County Commissioner Richard Kerr testifying to the character and integrity of certain defendants. Others claimed they had provided Casamayor with loans and other financial assistance and thus an explanation for his free-spending ways.

Detective Carroll Key called the allegations against him simply "lies."

Michael Cates went a step further, calling testimony for the prosecution "outrageous lies." The prosecution hit back, naturally, attempting to discredit as many defense witnesses as possible.

By May 21, 1985, closing arguments were underway in the landmark, 10-week trial. Prosecutor Michael Sullivan claimed that the conspiracy began with Casamayor's protection of a pot smuggling operation in 1978. It had grown in size and scope until the September 1983 arrest of Hector Serrano, corrupting other individuals and turning the Key West Police Department into a "criminal enterprise."

Defense lawyers countered that the prosecution's witnesses included "slugs, liars and lowlifes," and in the case of Serrano and Reynolds, "Princes of Industry" running a concern called "Coke, Inc. – The Real Thing." There was no seized cocaine admitted into evidence, they noted, just the word of "brain-toasted" addicts such as Reynolds.

'The Bubba Bust'

By May 28 both sides in the dramatic trial rested their cases. The proceedings had been exhausting. White Santeria powder had been found sprinkled on a courtroom bench. A car had been bombed. Residents of the Southernmost City held their breath awaiting the outcome.

■ ■ ■

On May 30, the verdicts were in – and they stunned longtime observers of local corruption. Not only were Casamayor and the other two cops found guilty of running a protection racket, but all the other defendants, save for Oneri Fleita and Leon Edwards, were convicted as well. The cops were all immediately fired from their city jobs and remanded to custody. Also held without bail were Michael Brito, Tony Diaz, Artie Brito and Michael and Janet Cates. Both husband and wife expected to be stripped of their licenses by the Florida Bar and state Realtors' association, respectively.

At the Aug. 7 sentencing, Casamayor, called a one-man "crime wave" by prosecutor O'Connor, was sentenced to 30 years in prison, while the two other former cops received 15 years each. Michael Cates drew a 15-year term and a $75,000 fine and his wife Janet 10 years and a $50,000 fine. Also sentenced were Antonio Diaz, 30 years; Artie Brito, 20 years; Buford Clark, Michael Clark, and John Roberts, 10 years each, and Carol Hardin, 5 years. Miguel Brito-Williams was sentenced a short time later to 25 years.

All contested their convictions, to no avail. On Feb. 23, 1988, the 11th Circuit Court of Appeals upheld the sentences, all of which have, by now, been served.

In the days following the trial, opinions of the outcome varied, with some still professing support for native son Casamayor.

"Where's the evidence?" Bahama Village resident Sam Jones asked *Miami Herald* reporter Chris Vaughn. "I don't believe all that hearsay. Where's the cocaine itself?"

For many Key Westers though, the results were definitive of a new, more transparent era in Key West public life – one in which official cor-

True Crime Stories of Key West and the Florida Keys, Vol. 2

ruption would no longer be tolerated either by Monroe County residents or the federal government.

"I think this means the big Bubbas won't be able to do whatever they want anymore," a Fausto's Food Palace customer told Vaughn. "They're finding out that Key West is part of the United States and they're going to be held responsible for what they do."

Tellingly, however, the man refused to give his name.

"It's still a small town," he said sheepishly . . . .

CLEANING HOUSE:

Following the embarrassing spectacle of the "Bubba Bust," the City of Key West hired new Key West Police Chief Tom Webster to clean up the department's image. Webster, who was the first chief trained at the FBI National Academy, was considered by many to be abrasive and aloof, but was able to rehabilitate the KWPD's image in the eyes of the public. He served from 1987-91.

'The Bubba Bust'

Photo courtesy of Nancy Klingener

Emmett Monroe Spencer, with cigarette, is uncuffed by Monroe County Sheriff's deputies during his August, 1960 trial at the county courthouse in Key West.

End of the Rainbow

'Dream Killer' Emmett Spencer crisscrossed the country on a wild crime spree with his sweetheart. It took Florida Keys lawmen to put an end to his twisted career....

End of the Rainbow

It sometimes seems like every criminal on the lam eventually makes it down to the Keys. Whether they're fleeing a jurisdiction where they're wanted, looking for a different place to set up shop and start a new life, or just using the island chain as a jump-off location to leave the country, the Keys, and especially Key West, are an inviting destination – sort of like a pot of gold at the end of a mostly two-lane, asphalt rainbow.

In fact, a huge chunk of the violent crime down here is committed by newly arrived drifters who are just passing through. This is the story of one such man; a maniacal criminal whose acts shocked even the experienced law enforcement agencies of Key West and the Florida Keys.

■ ■ ■

Early in the evening on April 15, 1960, Trooper John Cox of the Florida Highway Patrol was cruising his beat on a highway between Clermont and Leesburg in central Florida, when he was overtaken by a speeding Ford Galaxie. Cox pursued the vehicle for 10 miles before the Ford pulled over, revealing two men and a young woman inside. Cox ordered the male driver out of the car and demanded to see his license. The speeder called to the woman in the car to bring it out to him. Right off, Cox could see that the information on the license didn't match the driver and he said as much. Seeing that his bluff had been called, the driver grabbed the woman and backed away towards the car, using her as a shield. "Don't worry, dear," he said to the woman, "He will not shoot you."

Upon reaching the car, the driver shoved the female aside, jumped into the car and sped off in a cloud of dust. Cox and his new female passenger followed in hot pursuit with the policeman firing warning shots off into the humid spring night. Eventually, the Ford pulled over again as the driver struggled with his remaining passenger for control of a handgun. Winning the battle, the driver scurried from the car and fired a shot into the shoulder of Cox, who was approaching on foot to make the arrest. As the fugitive driver sped off yet again, the other male leapt from the car and rushed to the aid of the fallen officer. Unfazed by his injury, Cox and his two detainees pulled back onto the highway and joined in the chase with other cops responding to Cox's distress call.

At the outskirts of Leesburg the speeding Ford encountered two police roadblocks, crashing through the first one as the cops peppered the vehicle with bullets and buckshot. The Galaxie then T-boned a cruiser which was part of the second blockade, raining shards of glass down upon the officers and disfiguring one of them for life. Two other officers were critically injured in the carnage.

As the Ford's driver emerged from the wreckage, hands on top of his head, an unharmed kitten crept from the car as well and was taken into "protective custody" by an amateur photographer at the scene.

All three suspects were taken to Tavares County Jail as the cops tried to ascertain ownership of the obviously stolen car. A search of the Galaxie produced clothing that was much too large for any of the suspects, a typewriter, a television set, a dozen or so guns and hundreds of rounds of ammunition. A teletype exchange with the Monroe County Sheriff's Department revealed that the car belonged to the man listed on the bogus license, a Johnnie Thomas Keen, 57, of 1506 Seminary St., Key West.

A deputy was dispatched to the address, where he discovered Keene's lifeless body lying on a blood-soaked bed, his head brutally

At the time of the crime...

Just two days after the arrest of Spencer and Hampton the *Citizen* reported on another case with eerie parallels to the Spencer affair. On April 17, 1960 newlyweds Alvin and Barbara Table and their fugitive friend Billy Sees took off from Key West on an aquatic joyride aboard a stolen cabin cruiser. They ran aground in Elbow Cay in the Bahamas and spent five days in a lighthouse. Sees and Alvin Table then commandeered a passing Islamorada-based charter boat, killed its captain, Angus Boatwright, and left its crew, passengers — and Barbara Table — on the island. The two men headed towards Cuban waters with a U.S. Coast Guard plane flying overhead. After beaching east of Havana they were captured by Cuban authorities and eventually extradited to face justice in courts in both the Bahamas and the United States. Barbara Table described her ordeal as a "horrible dream."

End of the Rainbow

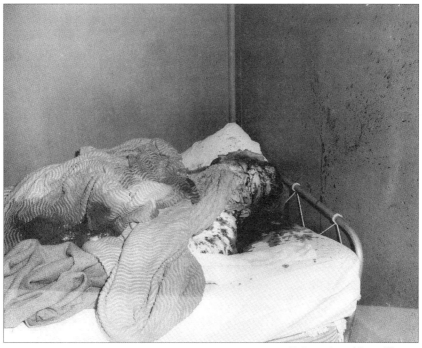

Photo courtesy of Nancy Klingener
The body of Spencer murder victim Johnnie Thomas Keen was discovered on April 15, 1960, on a bloody bed at 1506 Seminary St.

beaten to a pulp. Before long, deputies were dispatched to Leesburg to bring the trio back to Key West for questioning.

The driver of the Ford was identified as Emmett Monroe Spencer, 29, of Sandy Hook, Kentucky. His two traveling companions were Mary Katherine Hampton, also of Sandy Hook, and James L. Jobe, 23, of Nova Scotia, Canada, who claimed to have been picked up hitchhiking by Spencer and Hampton. Only Spencer had a criminal record. Hampton — who was seven-months pregnant with Spencer's child — had the "face of an angel," according to one of the cops. Jobe, who had been working at his job in the Middle Keys town of Marathon earlier in the day, seemed to have merely hitched a ride with the wrong driver.

But just who was Emmett Spencer and how and why had he ended up linked to such a despicable murder?

■ ■ ■

Described as a "bad boy from his early youth," by Sandy Hook Sheriff Bill Manning, Spencer had been convicted at 17 of involuntary manslaughter for the card game shooting of a La Grange, Kentucky doctor and sentenced to 10 years in state prison. He escaped but was recaptured in West Virginia. Later paroled, Spencer was arrested again for forgery and issuing bad checks. By 1959 he had been paroled a second time, but at the time of his Leesburg arrest police were seeking Spencer for breaking the terms of that parole.`

During his Key West interrogation Spencer blamed the Keen murder on Jobe. Alibi witnesses were procured, however, and on May 25 Spencer was indicted for the savage slaying as well as grand larceny for the robbery of a trailer on Grassy Key, north of Marathon. Neither Jobe nor Hampton was indicted, but both cooled their heels in the Monroe County Jail under $2,500 bond each for the duration of Spencer's trial. (Hampton had initially been charged with murder and grand larceny, but these charges were dropped in exchange for her testimony against her law-breaking boyfriend, Spencer.)

As questioning of Spencer continued, he told his captors about a series of dreams he'd had involving murders from Idaho to Florida. He led Monroe County Sheriff's Investigator Bobby Brown to a mangrove thicket on Big Coppitt Key where the cops discovered the badly decomposing body of Leon C. "Shorty" Hammel, 45, of Jacksonville. Spencer admitted to killing Hammel and then outlined other murderous "dreams" he'd had, including one involving Virginia Tomlinson of Jacksonville, whose body had been found May 6 near Vero Beach, Florida. That killing he blamed on "Shorty" Hammel.

Spencer was then linked to the murder of a college professor in Idaho, though he blamed the actual killing on a California traveling companion who was arrested shortly thereafter and charged with the murder.

Eventually, Spencer, Hampton and the other man were indicted for

End of the Rainbow

Photo courtesy of Nancy Klingener

Emmett Spencer led Monroe County sheriff's deputies to the decomposing body of Leon C. 'Shorty' Hammel on Big Coppitt Key.

the Idaho slaying and the *Key West Citizen* began referring to Spencer as the "Dream Killer."

■ ■ ■

On July 3, 1960, Mary Hampton, still in police custody in Key West, gave birth to a healthy baby boy. The authorities quickly stepped in and took custody of the child, intending to put it up for adoption.

Upon Hampton's return from the hospital, Investigator Brown began grilling her about Spencer and the grisly murders.

Hesitant at first, Hampton finally broke down and opened up.

She had met Spencer a year prior at a dance in Sandy Hook, she said. Together, the pair had traveled to California, where they met up with

Photo courtesy of Nancy Klingener

Spencer's former girlfriend Mary Hampton is led from the hospital following the birth of their son in July of 1960.

End of the Rainbow

a hillbilly musician named Roger Hall and his girlfriend "Bonnie." Like an evil version of "On The Road," the four embarked on a tour of West Coast states, financed with money from multiple robberies. At one point they found themselves in Idaho, where, she said, Hall and Spencer decided to find a motorist in a nice car to stick up. A man named John Hunt passed by the quartet and the hoodlums pulled him over at gunpoint.

As soon as he got out of his car, Hunt was beaten, shot to death and robbed of several hundred dollars in traveler's checks and other items.

Spencer then turned his car around and returned to California minus "Bonnie," who, Hampton said, had been ditched somewhere along the way.

Several weeks later, Spencer and Hampton were in Jacksonville, where they met up with "Shorty," and his girlfriend. As they headed south, Spencer and Shorty's girl began quarreling non-stop. When they reached Vero Beach, Spencer, who was wielding a knife, and Shorty ordered the woman out of the car and into some bushes. A short time later, the two men emerged, wiped their hands on some weeds, then got back into the car and headed south towards Key West.

Hampton took a deep breath and continued.

The trio had stopped for the night at a fishing camp in the Keys called Jo Jo's. Spencer and Shorty began drinking and wandered away from the cabin they had rented. They returned later with a man named J.M. Gallagher and continued to party. As the evening progressed, the three men left to find more whiskey, leaving Hampton to fall asleep by herself.

The next day, the drinking binge continued. As the sun began to set on the camp, Spencer came to the cabin and told Hampton to pack up as he was ready to leave. On the way out of the camp, Spencer beckoned Hampton inside a trailer where Gallagher lay passed out on a bed. Spencer stole the man's TV and radio and then pointed a gun at him.

"His face became distorted," Hampton recalled. "I had never seen such a look on a face before." Horrified, Hampton convinced Spencer to leave Gallagher alone and the couple got into their car and headed for Key West, picking up Shorty a few miles down the road.

At one point, Hampton said, the drunken Shorty put his hand on her knee "by accident." This enraged Spencer, who pulled over and ordered Shorty into the mangroves. Hampton heard some shots, then Spencer returned to the car – alone. The two then drove the rest of the way to Key West.

■ ■ ■

Emmett Spencer's trial for the first-degree murder of Seminary Street resident Johnnie Keen began on Aug. 22, 1960 before the jam-packed Key West courtroom of Circuit Court Judge Aquilino Lopez. Nellie White, who owned the apartment where Spencer and Hampton had stayed in Key West, identified the hammer found at the scene of the Keen killing as belonging to her brother.

When Hampton took the stand to testify against the father of her newborn son, a hush fell over the courtroom and Spencer didn't take his eyes off her for an hour and a half.

She said that Spencer had left their apartment with a gun and the hammer in his tool belt, returning a short time later with his pants torn.

"He was a big man," Spencer told her. "I hit him over the head and put him out of this world." He had torn his pants, Hampton said, jumping out of Keen's window following the murder.

Asked why she had not left him, Hampton replied that she "was afraid he would find me and kill me."

On the second day of the trial, Spencer took the stand in his own defense and told a very different story from his former girlfriend. First off, he blamed the murder of Virginia Tomlinson on Hampton and Shorty, who, conveniently enough, wasn't alive to refute the charge. He then claimed that Shorty had brought them all to Key West promising that his friend Johnnie Keen could get the two men jobs at the Navy yard. On their second day in Key West, Spencer said, Shorty told him he had killed Keen and the trio quickly blew town. Driving north near Big Coppitt Key, Spencer said that Hampton had professed her love for Shorty and announced that they would be going off together. Spencer stopped the car and Shorty came at him with a knife. He had shot the man in self-defense, Spencer said, and dumped his body in the mangroves.

Hampton was brought back for rebuttal testimony and called Spencer a liar.

He said, she said.

In his closing argument, Assistant State Attorney Albury entreated the jury to "show [Spencer] no sympathy. He has shown none to others. He is the most vicious criminal ever to come before this court."

It took the jury just one hour to bring back a guilty verdict against Spencer and recommend the death penalty.

As he was led from the courtroom Spencer turned to Sheriff's Investigator Bobby Brown and snarled "You're first on my list when I get out."

∎ ∎ ∎

"They got a saying on death row . . .
Either you get smart, or you get dead."
- **Emmett Spencer**, 1970

Immediately after he was found guilty of Keen's murder, Spencer's attorneys filed a motion for a new trial, alleging that the verdict was contrary to the law and the evidence inconclusive to establish first-degree murder.

On Aug. 30, 1960, Judge Lopez denied the motion and instead sentenced Spencer to death in the electric chair.

From that point on, the convicted killer focused all his energies on staying alive and trying to have his conviction overturned. He wasted no time, however, in turning the tables on Hampton, who was about to walk away from the whole mess a free woman: Spencer implicated her in a double murder in Louisiana, for which she eventually served five years, before lawyer F. Lee Bailey secured her release.

As for Spencer, the Kentucky illiterate with the seventh-grade education began giving himself a crash course on the law from his cell, located just 15 feet from the death chamber at the Raiford State Penitentiary.

For five years, staying alive became his obsession. Then, in 1965, the governor of Florida – and several court injunctions – temporarily halted all executions in the state.

In May of 1967, Spencer and his court-appointed lawyer presented a 16-page legal brief to a federal judge in Jacksonville containing no fewer than 40 complaints of violations of his constitutional rights from the time of his arrest to the time of his conviction in Key West. This bid for freedom was turned down, as were several others. But by the late 1960s, the Warren Supreme Court had issued several legal mandates regarding confession-taking and trial publicity that ultimately led to a review of Spencer's case before the very judge who had previously sentenced him to die. In January of 1970, Spencer and his lawyer Edward Worton returned to the Southernmost City – and Judge Aquilino Lopez – one last time.

On Jan. 31, 1970, following his hearing, Spencer called his parents for the first time in a decade and told them "I'm not going to die in the electric chair." Judge Lopez had set aside his original judgment and granted Spencer a new trial on condition that Spencer admit his guilt in the Keen slaying and agree to a life term for the crime. With credit for his time served, Spencer could have been eligible for parole, but that was considered unlikely as he still had murder holds on him in Florida and Idaho. With the death penalty off the table, though, Spencer had found the pot of gold in the city that had literally been the end of the road for his crime career.

■ ■ ■

After hanging up the phone with his parents, Spencer received a visitor: Bobby Brown, who by now had become sheriff of Monroe County.

"You've put on a little weight, Bobby," Spencer said to the man whose life he once threatened. "Yeah," Brown responded. "You've got a little gray."

"Well, anyway Bobby, I just wanted to say goodbye," Spencer said. "I'll probably never see you again. No hard feelings on my part."

End of the Rainbow

"Mine either," the sheriff responded.

With that, Brown turned and walked out of the Monroe County Jail and past the U.S. Highway 1 sign marking the "The End of the Rainbow."

"For Emmett Monroe Spencer, the end of the rainbow is an end to life in an 8 x 10-foot green and white cell on death row at the Florida State Prison and a sentence of life in prison," wrote *Citizen* reporter James McLendon. "Somehow, it does not seem at all like the end of the rainbow."

For innocent citizens coast-to-coast, however, Spencer's life sentence was a true pot of gold. 💰

IF IT BLEEDS, IT LEADS:

The diabolical saga of the handsome yet brutal Spencer and his beautiful girlfriend Hampton was considered salacious enough to be featured in the September 1960 issue of *Startling Detective* magazine. The pulpy publication's take on the tale was entitled "Devil's Rampage with a Green-Eyed Blonde." Coincidentally, the story of the murder of Capt. Angus Boatwright by Billy Sees described on page 112 of this book was featured in the same issue of Startling Detective, under the title "Killer Pirates Off Elbow Key."

True Crime Stories of Key West and the Florida Keys, Vol. 2

Photo courtesy of Monroe County Library

Circuit Court Judge Aquilino Lopez, right, and his wife Lillian, left, escort presidential candidate Adlai Stevenson during a trip to Key West in the 1950s.

The Shocking Death of Judge Aquilino Lopez

This long-time Key West judge was considered a giant of the legal profession. His bizarre death in 1971 left many friends and family members asking questions . . . .

The Shocking Death of Judge Aquilino Lopez

Around 8:30 on the morning of April 12, 1971, Circuit Court Judge Aquilino Lopez, Jr. and his wife Lillian left their home at 1426 Reynolds St., got into their car and drove to the post office to pick up the mail. The judge then dropped Lillian off at the beauty parlor and returned home.

Lopez went into his bedroom and scribbled a short note on the back of an envelope. Then he disrobed and hung his clothes in the closet.

The judge took an extension cord and peeled back the insulation, exposing a one-foot length of copper wire, which he wrapped around his left ankle. He then walked into his ensuite bathroom, locked the door behind him and placed the note on the top of the sink. Lopez filled the bathtub and sat on the edge with his feet – and the wire – dangling into the water. He then reached over and plugged the extension cord into a wall socket, sending 110 volts of raw power coursing through his body. The force of the power surge killed Lopez instantly and knocked him into the tub.

Or so the coroner would later say.

Two hours later the judge's wife, concerned that her husband had failed to pick her up at the salon, enlisted the aid of an electrician – who, by coincidence, was installing floodlights outside the Lopez house – to force open the bathroom door.

The devastating discovery of the dead judge lying face-up in his bathtub shocked Mrs. Lopez and the whole town. It also raised the suspicion of friends and family members who still refuse to believe that this respected and honorable man took his own life. Never mind the suicide note found in the bathroom which read, in part, "May God forgive me, Aquilino Lopez."

■ ■ ■

Circuit Court Judge Aquilino Lopez Jr. was a pillar of the community.

He was born on Jan. 9, 1910 in the town of Illano of Oviedo, Spain, the son of a successful Key West businessman, Aquilino Sr., and his Spanish bride, Generosa.

The family returned to Key West in 1921, where the bright and ambitious future judge quickly mastered English and generally excelled in his studies. He graduated with honors from Key West High School and earned his Bachelor of Law degree from the University of Florida. Lopez was called to the bar in June of 1933.

In the years that followed, Lopez served as county attorney, city attorney and as a judge of the 11th Judicial Circuit of Florida. In November of 1948, he was elected to the position of circuit court judge of Dade and Monroe counties. During his tenure, the district was split, but he remained at the helm of the newly created 16th Judicial Circuit and ended up serving as the senior jurist of Monroe County residents for a total of 26 years, until his death. During the course of his notable career, he was admitted to practice before the U.S. District Court, the U.S. Circuit Court of Appeals for the Fifth Circuit and the U.S. Court of Military Appeals. Among his many other accomplishments, he had sat on several occasions as a guest judge on the Florida Supreme Court.

It's difficult to list any important court cases in Monroe County during his tenure in which he was not involved in some way and he was proud of the fact that none of his decisions were later reversed on appeal.

Lopez' civic record was equally impressive. The devout Roman Catholic was a member of St. Mary's Star of the Sea Church and of the Knights of Columbus. He was president of the Navy League, a past president of the Key West Rotary Club and had served as a director of the Key West Chamber of Commerce for years. Lopez was a member of Elks Lodge No. 551 and was also known as a philanthropist, donating to the Key West Library and worthy students. His financial assistance was crucial in setting up the law library at the Monroe County Courthouse.

In short, this was a man who had earned the respect of his colleagues and the friendship of his neighbors and fellow citizens. At 61, he still had many years of life ahead of him and was, in fact, planning an extensive trip to Europe with his wife and friends later on that year.

What had happened?

■ ■ ■

On the morning of the judge's death, Dr. Herman K. Moore, who lived just a few blocks away, was tending to the orchids in his back yard when he heard the tragic announcement on the radio. Realizing that the judge's mother probably hadn't been told yet, he rushed over to her house and broke the sad news to her.

At the time of the crime...

On April 8, 1971, Monroe County Sheriff's deputies arrested John Pratt, aka "Brother John," the "leading guru" of the "Hippieville" community on Christmas Tree Island, for narcotics possession. Pratt, who was already incarcerated in the county jail for having improper equipment on his boat, asked authorities to check on his boat, as it had a leak. They did and discovered "a large quantity of marijuana, some hashish and a few pipes with the dregs of narcotics in the bowls."

The Shocking Death of Judge Aquilino Lopez

Moore, a *Key West Citizen* columnist who died in 2005, was to the medical profession in Key West what Lopez had been to the legal vocation and he was a good friend to the Lopez family as well as to the Ramos and Madden in-laws. As a doctor, he had faith in the Key West coroner, but his gut told him there was something wrong with its findings in this case.

"I know the coroner's inquest concluded that the death was a suicide," he wrote in a 1992 *Citizen* column. "[But] to this day, some family members believe the death was a homicide. There was just no reason for this popular and able jurist to end his own life."

Aside from the apparent lack of a motive, Moore had difficulty accepting the method his old friend supposedly used to kill himself.

"How a man who knew almost nothing about electricity and electrical repairs could lock the door to his bedroom, put an electric cord about his leg, get in the tub and then put the plug in the receptacle confounded all his friends."

The *Citizen* spoke for many on the day after Lopez' death when it asserted that "The mysterious death of Judge Lopez leaves most residents who knew him here completely baffled. Several prominent local people saw the judge just hours before his death Saturday and one said 'he appeared to be a completely happy man.'"

• • •

In the years since Judge Lopez' strange death, the case has remained officially closed, though not from a lack of trying on the part of friends like Moore to get it re-opened.

"There were rumors, but nothing significant has ever come to light to explain Aquilino's actions," Moore wrote in his 1992 column. "If anyone knows something I don't, I wish they would call me. I would take a vow of silence just to know the truth."

If only the walls could talk . . . .

> **THE TRAVELLING JUDGE:**
> According to former *Key West Citizen* reporter Frank Jacobson, Judge Lopez was known as "'The Traveling Judge,' in the old, true tradition of the 'circuit' jurist and he never, or hardly ever, shirked a call to sit on the bench in another court."

About the author

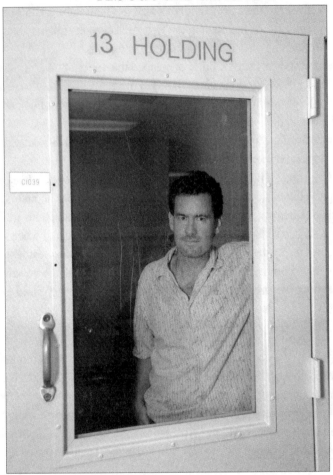

Photo by roboneal.com

Terry Schmida was born and raised in Toronto, Canada. He first visited Key West in 1976, at the age of 6, and relocated here permanently in 1995.

In 1997 Schmida became the crime reporter at the *Key West Citizen* newspaper. He currently serves as the paper's arts and entertainment, features and food editor. His first book, *True Crime Stories of Key West and the Florida Keys, Vol. 1*, was published in 2006.

Corrections/clarifications

This book is a work of non-fiction and every care has been taken in the research process to reflect accurate accounts of these historical events. Should you have compelling evidence to suggest that factual errors have been made in the telling of these stories, your input will be welcomed, and used in the editing of future editions of this book.

Also available from Phantom Press
www.phantompress.com

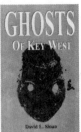

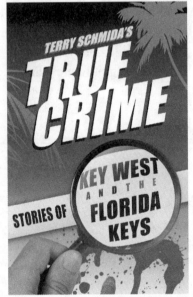